"One might think a book on French Calvinism is the stuff of historians, and perhaps to be put safely on the shelf with other records of its kind. That would be a grave mistake. As a matter of great significance both the essence of Calvinism and its uniquely French provenance have a decisive influence on the Christian faith of our times. The movement has gone beyond Collin Hansen's *Young, Restless and Reformed* to a far broader and arguably more commanding position. This volume will open up the many ways the undertaking has made its influence felt. It's a must read for anyone wishing to understand our times through a biblical lens."

—WILLIAM EDGAR, Professor Emeritus, Westminster Seminary

"*French Calvinism in the Sixteenth Century* offers a series of compelling biographies of leaders of the Reformation in France, which had one of the most influential yet tragic national traditions within the Protestant movement. I am happy to recommend this important book."

—THOMAS S. KIDD, Research Professor of Church History, Midwestern Baptist Theological Seminary

"Klauber and Davis deliver an essential introduction to the significant figures of French Reformed Protestantism of the sixteenth century and provide an honest and fair assessment of each. This volume will benefit both novices and scholars alike."

—DANIEL BORVAN, Pastor, Christ Reformed Church, Anaheim, California

"If you wonder how the history of the church can still be relevant today, I encourage you to read this book. With the authors, we follow main figures of French Calvinism in the sixteenth century, discovering the perseverance and faith of those faithful witnesses but even more the wonders of God's providential hand. Even though many lost their lives for their faith, God protected a church that is still alive today. The history of French Calvinism strengthens our faith and hope because our God is the same! In painting that history in a clear and vivid manner, the authors are rendering a great service to the church."

—YANNICK IMBERT, William Edgar Chair of Apologetics, Faculté Jean Calvin

"While the Huguenot (or French Reformed) movement largely died out by the eighteenth century because of fierce persecution, the theology of the French Calvinists lives on to this day. Through the life stories of men and women of God who lived their faith, wrote about their faith, and sealed their faith with blood, the authors use the medium of mini biography to show how a group of French laypeople and theologians helped shape early Reformed orthodoxy and piety. Prepare to meet an assortment of fascinating and theologically-astute men and women—such as Gillaume Farel, Marguerite de Navarre, John Calvin, Pierre Viret, and Theodore Beza—who challenge us through their lives, writings, and sufferings to live fully for the glory of the Triune God."

—JOEL R. BEEKE, Chancellor, Puritan Reformed Theological Seminary

French Calvinism in the Sixteenth Century

French Calvinism in the Sixteenth Century

A History in Biography

STEPHEN M. DAVIS
MARTIN I. KLAUBER

Foreword by Michael A. G. Haykin

WIPF & STOCK · Eugene, Oregon

FRENCH CALVINISM IN THE SIXTEENTH CENTURY
A History in Biography

Copyright © 2025 Stephen M. Davis and Martin I. Klauber. All rights reserved. Except for brief quotations in critical publications or reviews, no part of this book may be reproduced in any manner without prior written permission from the publisher. Write: Permissions, Wipf and Stock Publishers, 199 W. 8th Ave., Suite 3, Eugene, OR 97401.

Wipf & Stock
An Imprint of Wipf and Stock Publishers
199 W. 8th Ave., Suite 3
Eugene, OR 97401

www.wipfandstock.com

PAPERBACK ISBN: 979-8-3852-5684-6
HARDCOVER ISBN: 979-8-3852-5685-3
EBOOK ISBN: 979-8-3852-5686-0

09/04/25

Scripture quotations taken from The Holy Bible, New International Version®, NIV®. Copyright © 1973, 1978, 1984, 2011 by Biblica, Inc. Used with permission of Zondervan. All rights reserved worldwide. www.zondervan.com

Contents

Foreword by Michael A. G. Haykin — vii

Preface — ix

Introduction — 1

Chapter 1   Jacques Lefèvre d'Étaples (c. 1450–1537) — 17
Humanist Reformer
STEPHEN M. DAVIS

Chapter 2   Guillaume Farel (1489–1565) — 23
Defender of the Gospel
STEPHEN M. DAVIS

Chapter 3   Louis de Berquin (1490–1529) — 31
Christian Martyr
MARTIN I. KLAUBER

Chapter 4   Marguerite de Navarre (1492–1549) — 37
Guardian Angel
STEPHEN M. DAVIS

Chapter 5   Michel de L'Hôpital (c. 1505–73) — 42
Catholic Peacemaker
STEPHEN M. DAVIS

Chapter 6   John Calvin (1509–64) — 48
Reformed Theologian
MARTIN I. KLAUBER

CONTENTS

Chapter 7	Pierre Viret (1511–71) Pastor and Professor MARTIN I. KLAUBER	64
Chapter 8	Peter Ramus (1515–72) French Humanist MARTIN I. KLAUBER	70
Chapter 9	Gaspard de Coligny (1519–72) Huguenot Admiral MARTIN I. KLAUBER	77
Chapter 10	Théodore de Bèze (1519–1605) Reformer and Scholar STEPHEN M. DAVIS	84
Chapter 11	Pierre de la Place (c. 1520–72) Huguenot Martyr MARTIN I. KLAUBER	93
Chapter 12	Jeanne d'Albret (1528–72) Huguenot Queen STEPHEN M. DAVIS	103
Chapter 13	Louis I de Bourbon, Prince de Condé (1530–69) Huguenot General STEPHEN M. DAVIS	110
Chapter 14	Antoine de Chandieu (1534–91) Silver Horn STEPHEN M. DAVIS	118
Chapter 15	Henri IV (1553–1610) First Bourbon King STEPHEN M. DAVIS	126

Conclusion — 133
Chronology — 137
From the Same Authors — 141
Bibliography — 143
Index — 151

Foreword

As with so many other academic disciplines, there are a variety of ways of doing and writing history. The approach contained in this volume is one of the main ways that I have taught and written about history in the past three decades, namely, history through the prism of biography. Although I was trained as an intellectual historian in the late 1970s and early 1980s, my approach since the early 1990s has been to focus on the lives of people in all of their fullness and not simply engage with their ideas. This has entailed learning social and cultural history as well as the art of biography.

From the standpoint of Christian historiography, this approach makes sense, for the historical narratives in the Holy Scriptures reveal that God is deeply interested in people. And it was, after all, people for whom Christ lived and died, not ideas. To be sure, ideas—in Christian terms, dogma and doctrine—are important. But it is as they grip the minds and hearts of men and women that these ideas shape history. Without people to put them into practice, they would languish on the shelf, as it were!

The other thing I love about the book in your hands is its subject-matter: the French Calvinist tradition, or the history of the Huguenots. I would venture to say that most Anglophone evangelicals are completely ignorant about the knowledge of this tradition and story. Oh yes, they know of Calvin but nothing about his predecessors in the faith and his legacy among French-speaking believers in the sixteenth century. And this really is a shame, for this Reformed tradition has been enormously influential along a number of lines: exegetically and spiritually through the writings of men like Jacques Lefèvre d'Étaples and Pierre Ramus, as well as theologically, through the work of authors such as Théodore de Bèze and Antoine de Chandieu. Moreover, the lives narrated here are some of the

FOREWORD

most fascinating of the Reformation era. In the hands of a good director, a movie about Jeanne d'Albret or Gaspard de Coligny could be a blockbuster. But I venture to suggest that this book is just as good! A huge thank you to Stephen and Marty for this historical feast!

Michael A. G. Haykin, ThD, FRHistS
Dundas, Ontario

Preface

WE ARE DELIGHTED TO present these biographies on French Calvinism. The choice of the title was intentionally "French Calvinism" and not "French Calvinists." Most of the individuals featured in the following chapters were Reformed Protestants who identified with the teachings of Calvin. Several of the chapters, however, are devoted to individuals who supported aspects of the Reformation yet remained in the Catholic Church.

These fifteen biographies are selective and cover the period from the beginning of the Reformation in France in the early 1500s to the Edict of Nantes in 1598 under Henri IV. Understandably, there will be significant overlap between the chapters. This is not only intentional but also unavoidable, given that two authors wrote independently—and to provide historical context. Many of these individuals were contemporaries whose lives were intertwined in the same events: the *Affaire des Placards* (1534), the Conspiracy of Amboise (1560), the Colloquy of Poissy (1561), the Massacre of Huguenots at Vassy (1562), the Saint Bartholomew's Day Massacre (1572), the Wars of Religion (1562–1598), and the Edict of Nantes (1598). We have mostly used French orthography for proper names, with some exceptions for common names like John (Jean) Calvin.

We do not wish to give the impression that Calvinism was the only Reformation movement in France, although it was the most important in scope demographically and geographically. The teachings of Luther arrived in France before Calvin appeared on the scene, and early on, evangelicals were often called Lutherans by their opponents. Calvin's teachings soon eclipsed those of Luther, and Lutheranism became concentrated in regions of eastern France closest to Germany. Furthermore, not all aspects of traditional Calvinism in France were uncontested: controversies included

PREFACE

Calvin's role in the execution of Servetus and scandals like Guillaume Farel's marriage at the age of sixty-nine to a teenage girl. These people were saints in the biblical sense, set apart by God for salvation, and are examples of faith, courage, and godliness. However, they were not always saintly in their decisions and actions.

We hope that these biographical sketches will not only provide information but also stimulate reflection on the faith and failures of God's people. Even more, may the providential hand of God be seen in the triumphant and tragic events of this time.

Introduction

THE ORIGINS OF REFORMED Christianity in France are an overlooked subject, with many of the key figures generally unknown to the English-speaking public. This book presents brief biographies of significant individuals who contributed to the Reformation in sixteenth-century France. The story of the Reformation in France is marked by fascinating and tragic events, and the individuals who lived through it were often entangled in military conflicts, theological disputes, and political intrigues. Some embraced evangelical principles, sought reform, and rejected certain aspects of Roman Catholic doctrine and practices yet never left the Catholic Church. Notable figures include Marguerite de Navarre, Jacques Lefèvre d'Étaples, Louis de Berquin, and Michel de L'Hôpital. However, their contribution to the nascent Reformation in its early years was critical and substantial.

During the Reformation, the Protestant movement in France was characterized by its status as a persecuted minority throughout the sixteenth century. The predominance of Roman Catholicism within the French religious landscape has contributed to the neglect of significant contributions made by prominent theologians of the Reformed tradition who were of French origin. Often, these figures are mistakenly associated with Switzerland, Germany, or the Netherlands, even though many were refugees in these regions, fleeing a society embroiled in religious conflict. In the context of the Early Reformation, the French adherents to Protestantism were commonly designated as Huguenots, a term that emerged during the sixteenth century. The origins of the term "Huguenot" remain unclear, with various theories proposed. It may come from the Flemish term "Huisgenooten," meaning "housefellows," signifying those who gathered for Bible study. Alternatively, it may stem from the German word "Eidgenossen," or

INTRODUCTION

"confederates," referring to the Genevans united in their struggle for independence from the Duchy of Savoy. Regardless of its origin, the term "Huguenot" began to gain prominence following the Conspiracy of Amboise in 1560.[1]

The early years of the Reformation in France lagged somewhat behind its German and Lutheran counterparts, yet there was a direct and strong connection between the two. As early as the 1520s, a virtual flood of Lutheran writings were being widely read and discussed in France. In 1523, the Parlement[2] of Paris confiscated Lutheran works from booksellers and from a prominent humanist scholar in Paris, Louis de Berquin, whose biography is featured in this book.[3]

The emergence of humanism during the Renaissance initiated interactions with the original sources of intellectual and theological tradition, encapsulated in the phrase *ad fontes*. This movement advocated reexamining the Christian faith through the lens of the original biblical texts, written in Hebrew and Greek rather than the Latin Vulgate. Desiderius Erasmus (1467-1536) contributed significantly to this endeavor by publishing his first edition of the *Novum Testamentum* in 1516, utilizing superior Greek manuscripts inaccessible to Jerome when he composed the Vulgate. This pursuit was not limited to Erasmus; contemporaries in France also embraced a humanist approach, striving to produce more accurate and refined texts across both secular and theological literature. Erasmus's scholarship was characterized by what he termed "learned piety," a concept of faith emphasizing intellectual rigor, practical application, and a serious theological framework. The universities of the period emerged as fertile grounds for the proliferation of Lutheran ideas, bolstered by the influx of students from German territories, who formed a collective known as the "German nation" at institutions such as the University of Paris. Among the reformers of this era was Guillaume Briçonnet (1472-1534), who served as the bishop of Meaux beginning in 1515, following his tenure as abbot of Saint-Germain-des-Prés. Hailing from a wealthy lineage, Briçonnet distinguished himself as a reformer committed to ecclesiastical renewal. He visited each parish within his diocese and cultivated a network of like-minded reformers. His

---

1. Gray, "Origin of the Word Huguenot," 349-59.

2. *Parlements* were sovereign courts of justice throughout the kingdom formed by a group of specialists separate from the Royal Court from the time of the Capetians until the French Revolution (*Nouveau Petit Robert*, 1808).

3. Weiss, "Louis de Berquin," 180-81.

INTRODUCTION

father, also named Guillaume Briçonnet, was a prominent financier who, after the death of his wife, entered the clerical profession, ultimately ascending to the cardinalate and the archbishopric of Reims. Briçonnet, as abbot of Saint-Germain-des-Prés, sought to implement reforms within the monastery and assembled a group of reform-minded colleagues in 1507, who would later be recognized as part of the so-called Group of Meaux.[4]

In 1517, after establishing his residence in the diocese, he instituted a series of initiatives to strengthen the spiritual vitality of the diocese. His efforts primarily focused on enhancing clerical training to promote more scripturally based preaching and ensuring that clergy were residing within their respective parishes. To facilitate this educational reform, Briçonnet established a humanist intellectual community, inviting several distinguished scholars to collaborate, including Guillaume Farel, Gérard Roussel, and the renowned Jacques Lefèvre d'Étaples. These humanists engaged in serious study of the church fathers and the Scriptures while working towards ecclesiastical reform in a diocese approximately thirty miles east of Paris. Their reformative pursuits coincided with concerns prevalent among Lutheran reformers, particularly regarding the abuses associated with the sale of indulgences. This humanist circle began to question established Roman Catholic doctrines, most notably the doctrine of purgatory. Despite Briçonnet's official condemnation of Martin Luther's writings, he refrained from dismissing any clergy associated with these ideas, including Pierre Caroli, who would later clash with John Calvin. This complex interplay of reformative zeal, humanist scholarship, and ecclesiastical authority highlights the nuanced dynamics of early sixteenth-century religious reform in France.[5]

The pivotal connection between the humanist scholars of the early sixteenth century and the Reformation can be significantly attributed to Guillaume Farel (1489–1565). While studying at the University of Paris, Farel engaged with the esteemed monastic institution at Saint-Germain-des-Prés, where he cultivated a friendship with Lefèvre, a prominent educator at the school. Farel soon aligned himself with the Reformation, though not all of Lefèvre's protégés did so. Most, including Briçonnet, remained loyal to the Roman Catholic Church, hoping to reform it internally. Other notable followers of Lefèvre included Melchior Wolmar (1497–1560), a Greek professor at Bourges who later instructed John Calvin, and the

---

4. Vance, *Secrets*, 52.
5. Cameron, "Charges of Lutheranism," 119–49.

INTRODUCTION

eminent poet Clément Marot (1495–1544), known for his contributions to the French Psalter. Briçonnet and Lefèvre enjoyed the patronage of Marguerite de Valois, initially the Duchess of Angoulême, before marrying Henri d'Albret, the King of Navarre. Navarre encompassed territories in the Basque region, straddling northern Spain and southwestern France. Marguerite engaged in correspondence with Briçonnet, who espoused a form of Dionysian mysticism and exhibited support for evangelical doctrines. However, in 1525, the Parlement of Paris initiated a campaign against reformative efforts, prompting many reformers to flee Briçonnet's diocese; Marguerite provided refuge to several, including Lefèvre.[6]

On the morning of October 18, 1534, the citizens of Paris were greeted by the emergence of broadsheets bearing the title "True Articles on the Horrible, Great and Insufferable Abuses of the Papal Mass." This publication comprised four paragraphs of text that articulated significant grievances regarding the practices associated with the Papal Mass. The content of these broadsheets aroused fear within French Catholicism, but the placards reflected the growing discontent with papal authority and the institutional church.[7]

As a result of these placards, an atmosphere of fear of potential religious violence permeated Paris. These placards were not isolated to Paris; they were likewise discovered in five provincial towns and prominently displayed at the royal château in Amboise, notably pinned to the door of King François I's bedchamber and even placed within a bowl designated for his kerchief. Responding to the unrest, the king returned to Paris and established a special court charged with adjudicating cases of heresy, prompting the Parlement of Paris to apprehend suspects, many of whom faced execution by burning. On January 21, 1535, the king notably attended high mass at Notre Dame, where he seized the opportunity to encourage the populace to denounce heretics and their familial relations. The execution of six identified heretics took place publicly, followed by other executions. The climate of persecution compelled many, including the young reformer John Calvin, to seek refuge elsewhere. In 1557, François I's successor, Henri II, enhanced these measures by issuing the Edict of Compiègne, which threatened capital punishment for heresy.[8]

---

6. Cholakian and Cholakian, *Marguerite of Navarre*, 5.
7. Bruening, *Calvin's First Battleground*, 112–14.
8. Roelker, *One King, One Faith*, 231.

INTRODUCTION

On September 4, 1557, a mob armed with stones gathered outside a private residence on the rue Saint-Jacques in Paris, near the Sorbonne, where approximately four hundred Huguenots were engaged in worship. Among the attendees were numerous prominent members of the nobility and public officials. In response to the disturbance, government authorities intervened and arrested 132 individuals, including many women, who were subsequently imprisoned at the Grand Châtelet along the banks of the Seine River. By September 14, three of the accused, including a noble widow, were subjected to execution by burning at the stake.[9] Persecution forced many Huguenots to forsake the Catholic Church and flee the country. This included significant figures such as Pierre Viret and Théodore de Bèze, who sought refuge in Lausanne, and reformers John Calvin, who fled to Basel, and Guillaume Farel, who relocated to Geneva. Farel's most notable moment came in 1536 when he challenged Calvin, who was passing through Geneva on his way to Strasbourg, urging him to remain in Geneva to continue the work of reform. Farel expressed the severity of God's judgment should Calvin choose to depart. Calvin's theological contributions had a profound influence on the Huguenots. His *Institutes of the Christian Religion* became a foundational text for French Protestant thought. This included a covenantal theology wherein the New Testament sacraments of baptism and the Lord's Supper were seen as analogous to Old Testament rites such as circumcision and the Passover. The French Reformed Church followed Calvin's organizational structure, establishing the offices of pastor, elder, teacher, and deacon as outlined in his Ecclesiastical Ordinances (1541).[10]

Furthermore, the Academy of Geneva, established by Calvin in 1559, became an important institution for training pastors to minister in France. Official establishment of Reformed churches did not occur until the 1550s, as congregations were compelled to meet clandestinely to evade persecution, with missionaries from Geneva often utilizing pseudonyms for protection. The first Reformed church was founded in Paris in 1555, followed by another in Poitiers in 1557. The inaugural national synod convened in Paris in 1559 amid a reprieve from persecution, during which a Confession of Faith and a system of Discipline were adopted. This Confession drew heavily from the Genevan version and included a prefatory plea to King François II of France, imploring him to cease the oppression of Huguenots. The Confession articulates a straightforward exegesis of the doctrine of

9. Kelley, *Beginning of Ideology*, 91–92.
10. Manetsch, *Calvin's Company of Pastors*, 16–19.

5

INTRODUCTION

justification by faith. It delineates the completed work of Christ on the cross as the means to absolve believers from sin. This justification is imputed to individuals and is entirely devoid of human merit. The document posits that believers are regenerated upon justification by the Holy Spirit, who empowers them to live by godly principles. While affirming that the Old Testament law is fulfilled in Christ, the moral tenets of the law remain relevant as a guide for righteous living. Notably, the Confession refrains from espousing a developed doctrine of double predestination, asserting merely that God, in his mercy, calls some to salvation while leaving others in condemnation—a process entirely attributed to divine action apart from human deeds. The Confession explicitly repudiated various Roman Catholic practices, categorizing prayers to saints as insidious tools of Satan designed to divert believers from the true worship of God. It also condemned the doctrine of purgatory, viewing it as the foundation for additional Roman Catholic errors, including monastic vows, pilgrimages to holy sites such as Rome or Jerusalem, observance of feast and fast days, confession to a priest, and the sale of indulgences. The true church is characterized by the faithful preaching of the word of God and the proper administration of the sacraments. This led to the conclusion that the Roman Catholic Church was to be deemed a false church due to its neglect of the gospel and corruption of sacramental practice.[11]

The Protestant movement in France experienced significant growth, especially from the nobility and urban artisans. By the close of the century, following a series of devastating religious wars, about ten percent of France's population was Reformed. One of the factors contributing to the early success of the Reformed worship was its music, particularly the metrical adaptations of the Psalms by the eminent poet Clément Marot. Thousands of copies of printed Psalters were sold. These Psalms were essential in mobilizing troops during religious conflicts and facilitating corporate worship. The Psalter continued to evolve, particularly after 1560, when Théodore de Bèze expanded it to include all psalms, further entrenching its place in the Reformed liturgy and resistance efforts.[12]

Following the death of Henri II on July 10, 1559, from a jousting accident, the reins of power fell to his wife, Catherine de Medici, who came to be known as the Queen Mother. She was not powerful enough to control the noble factions who opposed each other on religious grounds. She had

---

11. Schaff, *Creeds of Christendom*, 3: 356–82.
12. Wursten, *Clément Marot and Religion*, 59–103.

four sons, three of whom would eventually accede to the French throne, and faced the difficult task of navigating the crown through political turmoil and factionalism. Her goal was to maintain the peace in the kingdom and minimize religious differences. Her faction has therefore often been labeled as *politique*. Her biggest threat came from François II's uncles; François, the Duke of Guise; and Charles, the Cardinal of Lorraine, who held extensive influence over the young king. They claimed descent from Charlemagne and ruled over the duchy of Lorraine. On the other side of the spectrum was Louis de Bourbon, Prince de Condé, who had converted to the Reformed faith after passing through Geneva and listening to a Protestant sermon. The Guise faction advocated the suppression of the so-called Protestant heresy in France and was leading royal policy in that direction.[13]

The power struggle that followed was primarily between three noble houses: the Guises, the Bourbons, and the Montmorencys, led by Constable Anne de Montmorency. The question of religion significantly reinforced these rivalries, making any prospect of enduring peace increasingly difficult. At the heart of the monarchy's authority lay the principle encapsulated in the maxim *une foi, une loi, un roi* (one faith, one law, one king), which underscored the sacral nature of the *Rex Christianissimus*, or the most Christian king of France. This assertion affirmed the unity of faith and governance and reflected the profound intertwining of religious and royal legitimacy during this critical juncture in French history.[14]

The control exercised by the Guise family over the French monarchy provoked significant alarm among various factions within the Protestant community, particularly among the followers of Louis de Bourbon, younger brother to Antoine de Bourbon. Condé emerged as a supporter of a plan aimed at liberating King François II from the influence of the Guises. However, the challenge of such a conspiracy involved multiple actors, thereby increasing the risk of leaking information. This attempt culminated at the Château d'Amboise on the banks of the Loire River on March 17, 1560, when Jean du Barry, seigneur de la Renaudie, with several hundred armed supporters, including some members of the nobility, tried to attack the castle. The effort was thwarted by forces commanded by the Duke of Guise, who had received advanced intelligence regarding the plot. In the ensuing conflict, Barry was captured and subsequently executed by drawing and

---

13. On the life and career of Catherine de Medici, see Céline Borello, *Catherine de Médicis*.

14. Holt, *French Wars of Religion*, 39–40.

INTRODUCTION

quartering, while between 1,200 and 1,500 of his followers met a similar fate, their bodies displayed as a grim warning on hooks along the castle walls or from nearby trees for public viewing. This event, now referred to as the Conspiracy of Amboise, was backed by Condé; however, it faced opposition from prominent figures within the Geneva Protestant community, notably John Calvin, who sought to dissuade involvement in the plot. Condé was apprehended in October 1560 following the conspiracy for his engagement in the endeavor. Some historians posit that he faced imminent execution, a fate which was averted by the untimely death of King François II in December 1560 due to an ear abscess. The subsequent ascension of Charles IX, François's younger brother, who was only ten years old, allowed Catherine de Medici to gain control of the council, displacing the Guises from power and facilitating Condé's release from imprisonment.[15]

In 1561, the Queen Mother adopted a stance of moderation that was met with considerable discontent among the Guise faction. She appointed Antoine, King of Navarre, who was positioned as the first prince of the blood (*prince du sang*) and thus held a legitimate claim to the regency, as Lieutenant-General of the realm.[16] This role placed him second in military command, subordinate only to Constable Anne de Montmorency. Additionally, she brought Gaspard de Coligny, a Huguenot and nephew of Montmorency, onto the royal council; notably, Coligny had refrained from supporting the Conspiracy of Amboise. In reaction to these political maneuvers, on Easter Sunday of 1561, François de Guise; Anne de Montmorency; and Jacques d'Ablon, the Marshal of St. André, convened to form what would come to be known as the "triumvirate." This coalition was dedicated to the defense of the Roman Catholic faith, supported by the interests of Philippe II of Spain.[17]

On April 19, Catherine de Medici responded by issuing an edict at Fontainebleau, allowing for private worship within their homes. However, the Protestant community sought permission to construct church buildings and the right to conduct public worship. In contrast, the royal council and the Parlement of Paris issued a countermand that prohibited even private worship and established a general amnesty for prior infractions of

---

15. Holt, *French Wars of Religion*, 44–45.

16. A *prince du sang* belonged to a branch of the royal family, even if not part of the reigning dynasty (*Nouveau Petit Robert*, 2022).

17. Carroll, *Noble Power During the French Wars of Religion*, 106–7.

religious regulations.[18] In response, Catherine de Medici, with the support of Chancellor Michel de L'Hôpital, convened the Colloquy of Poissy in September 1561 as a potential ground for theological compromise. L'Hôpital emerged as a sympathetic figure due to his role in ensuring the registration of the Edict of Romorantin by the Parlement of Paris, which sought to protect suspected heretics from the secret proceedings of the Inquisition. His underlying motivation was to promote a comprehensive reform of the French church to achieve unity between the Reformed and Roman Catholic factions.[19]

Additionally, L'Hôpital was instrumental in forming a council of notables to facilitate the convening of the Estates-General,[20] which ultimately took place following the death of François II. The subsequent endorsement by the new monarch, Charles IX, along with Catherine de Medici, laid the groundwork for both the Colloquy of Poissy and the Edict of Saint-Germain in 1562. However, L'Hôpital faced considerable opposition from the papal legate, Ippolito d'Este, primarily due to his critical stance on the authority of the Council of Trent and his Gallican views regarding royal power.[21] Tensions also arose with the Guise faction, particularly with the Cardinal of Lorraine, concerned about the potential consequences of enforcing the decrees of Trent on the fragile peace established with the Protestant community in France.[22]

At the Colloquy of Poissy, Théodore de Bèze and Peter Martyr Vermigli led a contingent of twelve Protestant theologians. In contrast, the Roman Catholics were represented by six cardinals and thirty-eight bishops and archbishops. Charles IX and the royal family's presence highlighted the proceedings' importance. Bèze endeavored to elucidate points of potential agreement. However, he provocatively asserted that Christ's body "is as far away from the bread and wine as the highest heavens are from the earth," prompting the assembly of prelates to exclaim "*blasphemavit*," indicative of their indignation. The situation was further complicated by the arrival of

---

18. Knecht, *French Religious Wars*, 30.

19. Nugent, *Ecumenism in the Age of the Reformation*, 98–105.

20. Estates-General (*États-Généraux*) were assemblies convened by the king composed of clergy, nobility, and commoners to provide counsel or vote on subsidies (*Nouveau Petit Robert*, 942).

21. The Gallican wing of the French Church sought greater autonomy from the Holy See; the Ultramontane faction supported the traditional position of the absolute authority of the pope (*Nouveau Petit Robert*, 1125, 2652).

22. Buisson, *Michel de L'Hospital*, 12; Crouzet, *Sagesse et le malheur*, 410.

INTRODUCTION

the papal legate Ippolito d'Este, the Archbishop of Ferrara, along with Diego Laynez, the General Superior of the Jesuit order, who sought to undermine any agreement. Despite efforts to reconcile the factions, it became increasingly evident that a consensus was unattainable, and the colloquy failed.[23] In January 1562, the French crown issued the Edict of Saint-Germain, also known as the Edict of January, that conferred upon Protestants the right to conduct peaceful worship services in rural areas beyond the confines of urban centers. While the edict specifically forbade the raising of arms and the observance of religious rituals during nighttime, for fear of armed insurrection, it represented a significant advancement for the Huguenots. However, the Parlement of Paris resisted by delaying the registration of the edict, necessitating a formal royal command from the young king to compel compliance, which the parlement ultimately executed in March 1562, albeit reluctantly.[24]

The Massacre of Vassy marked the escalation of the conflict on March 1, 1562. François, the Duke of Guise, accompanied by his entourage, was en route to Sunday Mass near his estate in northeastern France. Upon encountering a group of Huguenots engaged in worship within a barn, the duke attempted to force entry. In response, the Huguenots resisted, resulting in a violent confrontation during which stones were hurled, and the duke sustained injuries. In retaliation, he ordered the barn to be set ablaze, leading to the deaths of sixty-three worshipers and injuries to over one hundred others. The massacre elicited a range of responses among Protestant communities, from profound shock to intense outrage, prompting many Huguenot nobles to organize militarily out of fear for their safety. Leadership in this mobilization fell to figures such as Admiral Gaspard de Coligny and Louis, Prince de Condé. A series of military conflicts ensued that lasted until 1598.[25]

The Queen Mother endeavored to reconcile the divisions between the contending factions by orchestrating the marriage of the Protestant leader Henri de Navarre to her daughter, Margaret de Valois. This union was intended to ally the Huguenot faction and the royal house. A significant area of concern stemmed from the rhetoric found in Protestant publications, which suggested a growing dissent against the monarchy and promoted notions of popular sovereignty. Notably, Calvin, in his *Readings of the Prophet Daniel*

---

23. Nugent, *Ecumenism in the Age of the Reformation*, 98–105.
24. Daussy, *Parti huguenot*, 276–77.
25. Knecht, *French Religious Wars*, 80–84.

INTRODUCTION

(1561), posited that lesser magistrates had the authority to resist a tyrannical ruler and asserted that kings who disobeyed divine commandments forfeited their divinely sanctioned "worldly power." The predominantly Catholic population of Paris was particularly agitated for various reasons beyond the impending nuptials. In December 1571, a cross that had been erected on a stone pyramid at the site of the residence of the Huguenot Philippe de Gastines, who had been executed and whose home was set ablaze by a mob, was relocated to a cemetery. Gastines and his son, Richard, had been accused of conducting illicit worship services at their residence and were executed in July of 1569. The cross represented a symbol of purification for a location deemed tainted by the observance of the Protestant version of the Lord's Supper. The nocturnal removal of the cross by royal authorities incited riots that resulted in approximately fifty fatalities.[26]

Many among the Protestant nobility came to Paris to attend the nuptials on August 18, 1572. Coligny and other Protestant nobles stayed in Paris after the wedding to discuss with the king some improvements to the Peace of Saint-Germain. On the way back from the Louvre, Coligny was shot by a would-be assassin from the upper window of a house on August 22. He survived and the king promised to bring the perpetrators to justice. As a result, many in the capital feared reprisals, especially since Coligny's brother-in-law commanded about four thousand troops stationed outside the city. The royal council met on Saturday, August 23, and unanimously decided that it was time to eliminate Coligny once and for all. Historians have long questioned who was ultimately behind the plot to assassinate Coligny. Some point to the Guise family since they owned the house from which the shot had been fired. Others argue that the Queen Mother was behind the plot. Guise himself joined the entourage of a group of around a hundred individuals that murdered Coligny on his sickbed that evening and threw his body onto the street below. Then the crowd below cut off his genitals, his hands, and his head, and dumped the corpse into the Seine.[27]

The orchestrated attack extended beyond the confines of Coligny's residence, as the monarch mandated the mobilization of the city militia to secure the streets during the impending nocturnal assault against several dozen members of the Huguenot nobility who remained within the urban center. The subsequent murders, however, incited widespread popular reprisals targeting scores of Huguenots on the morning of August 24,

26. Diefendorf, *Beneath the Cross*, 83–86.
27. Diefendorf, *Beneath the Cross*, 93; Crouzet, *Nuit de la Saint-Barthélemy*, 135.

INTRODUCTION

known as St. Bartholomew's Day, with hosts of violent acts persisting for three days. These attacks were predominantly carried out by the general populace. Many participants believed that they were fulfilling the king's will, suggesting that the motivations were not limited to religious hatred but also included a sense of civic duty. Denis Crouzet has elucidated the distinctions between violence instigated by the crown and that perpetrated by the populace, asserting that the former was primarily motivated by a desire to safeguard the sacral integrity of the monarchy against what the crown identified as the revolutionary inclinations of the Reformed. In contrast, the violence emanating from the population was rooted in a conviction to fulfill divine will by purging the city of perceived heretics.[28] When the three days of pillage had concluded, about three thousand Huguenots had been killed.[29]

The violence then extended to various French provinces over six weeks, impacting twelve cities that were home to a significant Protestant minority. Approximately 3,000 to 8,000 Huguenots, and potentially more, were killed in locations including Orléans, La Charité, Meaux, Bourges, Saumur, Angers, Lyon, Troyes, Rouen, Bordeaux, Toulouse, and Gaillac. Significantly, the Protestants had previously controlled seven of these cities, even though they did not constitute most of the local population. The massacres developed later, in some instances not until October. Many perpetrators believed they were acting under the king's directives.[30] The impact of the massacre on the Protestant movement extended well beyond the immediate casualties. Many Huguenots chose to convert to Roman Catholicism for self-preservation. For instance, in Rouen, the Protestant population experienced a drastic decline, from approximately 16,500 to around 3,000.[31]

On May 30, 1574, Charles IX died from tuberculosis, leading his younger brother, Henri, Duke of Anjou, to become Henri III of France. There was considerable expectation that he would produce a legitimate heir to solidify the continuity of the Valois dynasty. Following Henri III in the line of succession were his younger brother, François, Duke of Alençon, and the Protestant Henri de Navarre. Both individuals were subjected to

---

28. Crouzet, *Dieu en ses royaumes*, 427–36. See also Crouzet, *Guerriers de Dieu*, 14–120.
29. Jouanna, *Saint Bartholomew's Day Massacre*, 3.
30. Jouanna, *Saint Bartholomew's Day Massacre*, 143–44.
31. Benedict, "St. Bartholomew's Day Massacre," 205–25.

INTRODUCTION

close surveillance at the royal court, reflecting the precarious nature of succession during this tumultuous period.[32]

The king encountered significant pressure from the recently established Catholic League, aimed at eradicating Protestantism from France. The Catholic League enjoyed widespread nationwide support, drawing from various confraternities that united in what many perceived as a crusade against heresy. Within the league, some regarded the king as insufficiently resolute against the perceived adversary and a *politique* lacking firm religious convictions. Consequently, they proposed the potential replacement of the king with a more devout figure, such as the Duke of Guise.[33]

In 1584, the death of the heir apparent to the French throne, the Duke of Anjou, at the age of twenty-nine from tuberculosis, created a significant political crisis. With King Henri III having no legitimate heirs, the succession would inevitably pass to the Protestant Henri de Navarre by Salic law. This prospect was intolerable to the Duke of Guise, who subsequently allied with King Philip II of Spain, securing annual financial support for the Catholic League. In response, Henri III consented to the Treaty of Nemours on July 7, 1585, effectively disinheriting Henri de Navarre. The treaty also mandated the removal of all Protestants from positions of authority within the government, conferred substantial control over northeastern France to the Duke of Guise, and prohibited the Reformed faith throughout the realm, establishing Roman Catholicism as the sole state religion.[34]

The league was growing more and more dissatisfied with Henri III's ability to rule effectively. This tension culminated in the event known as the Day of the Barricades in Paris on May 12, 1588. As a result of this uprising, the king left the city. Following this upheaval, Paris and the French government fell under the control of the Committee of Sixteen, a body established through representatives chosen from sixteen quartiers of Paris. To mediate on behalf of her son, the Queen Mother sought to exert her influence. However, her limited negotiating power forced her to acquiesce to the demands of the Guise faction. Consequently, she was obliged to announce Charles, Cardinal of Bourbon, as the legitimate heir to the throne, while Henri of Guise was appointed Lieutenant-General of the realm.[35]

32. Holt, *Duke of Anjou*, 42–44.
33. Holt, *French Wars of Religion*, 126–27.
34. Knecht, *French Religious Wars*, 222.
35. Greengrass, *France in the Age of Henri IV*, 43–54.

INTRODUCTION

The king recognized the rise of the power of the Guise faction as a threat to his rule. He convened a meeting of the Estates-General at Blois in 1588. During these proceedings, the king's apprehensions regarding the Guise faction's control over the Third Estate intensified.³⁶ On December 23, 1588, at the royal residence in Blois, he invited the cardinal and the Duke of Guise for a private audience. Upon the duke's entry into the king's chamber, he was assassinated by the monarch's bodyguards. Subsequently, the cardinal was arrested, imprisoned, and ultimately met the same fate.³⁷ The murder of the Guise brothers provoked significant anger throughout the country, resulting in a split between the monarchy and the Catholic League. In addition, the Parlement of Paris ruled that the king's conduct was illegal, leading many to argue that his actions were so outrageous that he had given up his claim to the throne. Making matters worse, the Queen Mother, Catherine de Medici, died on January 5, 1589. Consequently, an unexpected alliance emerged between Henri III and Henri de Navarre.³⁸

Charles of Lorraine, the Duke of Mayenne and brother to the assassinated Guises, ascended to leadership of the Catholic League. He mobilized troops to seize control of Paris, a city where he enjoyed considerable popularity. The league also actively disseminated anti-royalist propaganda, and the Sorbonne endorsed the radical notion that the reigning monarch could be deposed. This atmosphere of dissent culminated in the assassination of King Henri III on January 7, 1589, when Jacques Clément, a Dominican friar, fatally stabbed the king. As he succumbed to his injuries, Henri III summoned Henri de Navarre, designating him as his successor, and implored the Huguenot leader to embrace Catholicism.³⁹ As the successor to the French throne by Salic law, Henri de Navarre presented a significant challenge in establishing governmental authority over a divided country; despite his formal designation as Henri IV, the transition to actual governance required overcoming formidable obstacles, particularly the opposition posed by the Catholic League.⁴⁰

---

36. The Third Estate (*le tiers-état*) was one of three pre-revolutionary orders (*les trois états*) of the Estates-General, along with the nobility and the clergy. The Third Estate represented the majority of French people.

37. Holt, *French Wars of Religion*, 129–30.

38. Holt, *French Wars of Religion*, 131–35.

39. Knecht, *Hero or Tyrant*, 298–303.

40. Holt, *French Wars of Religion*, 136–41.

INTRODUCTION

Despite consistent efforts to seize the city of Paris between 1590 and 1592, Henri IV recognized that only his conversion to Roman Catholicism could effectively rally public sentiment in Paris and undermine the influence of the league. Although Henri ultimately renounced his Reformed faith in 1593 and was officially received into Roman Catholic communion, it is unlikely that he ever made the purported statement "Paris is worth a Mass." This assertion appears to be a product of propaganda disseminated by the Leaguers, who sought to portray his conversion as a disingenuous political maneuver.

The negotiation of a settlement to appease the Huguenots encountered delays, necessitating Henri IV to exercise caution in his dealings with his former co-religionists to avoid alienating the Roman Catholic populace. The Edict of Nantes was not officially proclaimed until August 1598. Despite Henri IV's official conversion to Catholicism, many questioned his true beliefs and saw his concessions as an endorsement of what they believed were heretical Protestant doctrines. The assassination of Henri IV in 1610 by François Ravaillac, a radical Roman Catholic, initiated a gradual erosion of Huguenot privileges during the seventeenth century under the reigns of Louis XIII and Louis XIV. This decline ultimately culminated in the Revocation of the Edict of Nantes in 1685, which dealt a critical blow to the religious rights and civil liberties of the Huguenot population in France.[41]

---

41. Holt, *French Wars of Religion*, 166–73.

Chapter 1

Jacques Lefèvre d'Étaples (c. 1450–1537)
Humanist Reformer

STEPHEN M. DAVIS

THE FRENCH HISTORIAN JEAN-HENRI Merle d'Aubigné wrote that "Christianity and the Reformation are the two greatest revolutions of history . . . a monk spoke and in half of Europe the power of [the Church of Rome] collapsed."[1] Jacques Lefèvre d'Étaples, a son of the Catholic Church, prepared the way for the second revolution in France. He was a man of immense culture with the soul of a missionary and a passion for putting the Scriptures in the language of the people.

As the Reformation dawned in 1517, Lefèvre was already over fifty years old, with as much authority and notoriety as Desiderius Erasmus (c. 1466–1536). Erasmus and Martin Luther (1483–1546) were representatives of two approaches to the reformation of the Catholic Church. Erasmus's approach was characterized by prudence, Luther's by resolution and action. Lefèvre adopted the first approach and believed, as did Erasmus, that reform was possible within the church without a rupture. Although he never officially left the Catholic Church, Lefèvre grasped evangelical truth before Luther and Calvin appeared on the scene.[2]

---

1. D'Aubigné, *Histoire de la Réformation*, 2–3.
2. Miquel, *Guerres de religion*, 46.

Jacques Lefèvre was born between 1450 and 1455 in Étaples, in the region of Picardy, and was greatly influenced by the great Dutch humanist Erasmus, who published his critical edition of the New Testament in Greek in 1516.[3] Humanism was characterized by a return to classical authors, the study of Greek and Latin, and biblical scholarship focusing on the critical study of Hebrew and Greek texts. Lefèvre became a Christian humanist and a Renaissance thinker. He followed the French armies into Italy to meet the great savants including the renowned Renaissance nobleman and philosopher, Giovanni Pico della Mirandola (1463–1494).[4]

Lefèvre taught philosophy at the University of Paris from 1490 to 1508 and was known for his extreme religious devotion in attending the Mass and processions and praying for hours at the feet of statues of Mary. He experienced a religious crisis as early as 1505. Through his study and reading of the Bible, his eyes were gradually opened to the biblical truth of justification by faith. At the time of the publication of his Latin version of the Fivefold Psalter (*Psalterium quintuplex*) in 1509, "even though he had not yet said farewell to the ancient philosophers and the medieval mystics, the appearance of this work gave notice that from now on the Bible and the propagation of its teachings would occupy the central position in his life."[5] His evangelical commentary on the Pauline Epistles in 1512 purportedly influenced Luther, and although the exact date of his understanding of justification is debated, his life and ministry serve as a reminder that God was at work in different places and times before Luther came on the scene.[6] By 1522, the publication of his commentary on the Gospels clearly showed that he "had decisively rejected any notion that the performance of penances possessed meritorious efficacy for the canceling or expiation of sins committed by baptized persons."[7]

Bishop Guillaume Briçonnet II (1472–1534), Count of Montbrun, was sent to Rome in 1516 by the French king François I (r. 1515–47) to negotiate the Concordat of Bologna with Pope Leo X (p. 1513–21). After spending time in Rome, Briçonnet departed with a diminished regard for the papacy. However, he did not wish to separate from Rome completely. When he returned to his diocese, he was appalled by the disorder that reigned

---

3. D'Aubigné, *Histoire de la Réformation*, 113.
4. Miquel, *Guerres de religion*, 47.
5. Hughes, *Lefèvre*, 53.
6. Félice, *Histoire des protestants*, 25.
7. Hughes, *Lefèvre*, 82.

and sought to put an end to the scandalous behavior of many priests. He hired preachers in 1518 and sent them throughout his parishes to evangelize Catholics who had fallen away from the church in their commitment to religious observances. A year later, with discouraging results, Briçonnet decided to train new priests and pursue his project of reform. He held the conviction that the reformation of customs and mores was useless apart from a transformation of the inner person.[8]

Briçonnet had been in contact with Lefèvre since 1505. It was only natural that he invited Lefèvre to Meaux in 1521 to spearhead reformation initiatives within the Catholic Church. This was four years after Luther posted his ninety-five theses against indulgences and the same year that Luther was summoned before the Diet of Worms. Guillaume Farel joined Lefèvre, and as a result of their activities and teaching, Meaux became the principal place of activity for the "evangelicals" and a group known as the Circle of Meaux. In the eyes of some, Lefèvre appeared factious and dangerous and was surveilled by his adversaries. He raised the question on which all future Reformers would take a position—the relationship between faith and works in the justification of sinners. Lefèvre exhorted Christians to read and meditate on the Gospels and opposed the church's position that commoners could never sound the sublime depths of Scripture.[9] He held other views that were incompatible with Catholic teaching. His view of the Eucharist "appeared to draw close to the commemorative teaching commonly associated with Zwingli."[10] He believed that in Jas 5:14–16, "James was not proposing extreme unction for those who were passing from this life to the next, but anointing with confession of sins and prayer for healing."[11] Controversy dogged him after his 1518 treatise showing that "the Mary Magdalene celebrated in the church calendar was a figure compounded of three different women": Mary of Bethany (Luke 10:39), Mary Magdalene (Luke 8:2), and "the unnamed woman who had been forgiven much and had anointed Christ's feet with ointment (Luke 7:37ff)."[12]

Although adversaries at the Faculty of Theology of Paris treated Lefèvre with contempt, the opposition did not stop Parisian students from visiting Meaux. There were notable visitors at Meaux such as Marguerite

---

8. Miquel, *Guerres de religion*, 40–46.
9. Garrisson, *Histoire des protestants*, 33.
10. Hughes, *Lefèvre*, 87.
11. Hughes, *Lefèvre*, 93.
12. Hughes, *Lefèvre*, 118–19.

de Navarre (1492–1549) and her queen mother, Louise de Savoie.[13] Lefèvre and the Circle of Meaux engaged in their missionary work throughout the region. They argued for a return to apostolic teaching and denounced the veneration of saints and the sale of indulgences. Lefèvre translated and published the four Gospels in 1522 and later wrote a commentary on them. The bishop encouraged him to distribute the Gospels at no charge to the poor. Sundays and holidays were consecrated to the study of the Gospels, which made their way into the fields and workshops of the region. As people took the teaching seriously, there was also a reformation of morals, which became evident in daily life. Day laborers from Picardy and other places who came into the region of Meaux at harvest time returned to their homes with the Gospels and the teachings they heard preached. The influence was so great that a proverb circulated in France during the first half of the sixteenth century which designated any adversaries of Rome as "heretics of Meaux."[14] Lefèvre then translated the entire New and Old Testaments into French. When Lutheran teachings were condemned by the Faculty of Theology in 1521, the school at Meaux was placed under suspicion, which opened the way for an era of violence.[15]

After Luther's excommunication by Pope Leo X in 1521, many friends of Lefèvre defected and returned to the safety of the church. Jacques Pauvent, a disciple of Lefèvre, was accused of writing pamphlets against purgatory, the invocation of the Virgin and saints, and holy water. The news spread, the search for heretics intensified, and the Circle of Meaux was warned that they no longer enjoyed official protection. More arrests followed, and Lefèvre fled in exile to Strasbourg. The persecution intensified in 1533 when François I met with Pope Clement VII (p. 1523–34) at Marseilles to arrange the marriage between his son, the future King Henri II, with Catherine de Medici, the pope's niece.[16]

Two events changed the course of French Reformation history and dashed any hope for reform in the Catholic Church. These challenges to Rome's religious hegemony led to increasing hostilities and repression and were foreboding precursors to the Wars of Religion. The first event took place at the beginning of the academic year at the University of Paris in 1533. In his opening remarks, the rector Nicolas Cop, a friend of John

---

13. Stéphan, *Épopée huguenote*, 36–37.
14. Félice, *Histoire des protestants*, 28.
15. Stéphan, *Épopée huguenote*, 25–26.
16. Miquel, *Guerres de religion*, 58–59

Calvin, defended the need for reform within the church in his sermon on the Beatitudes. It was understood as an attack on church authority, and a scandal broke out. Calvin was suspected of having a part in preparing the sermon. He and Cop fled to southwestern France under the protection of Marguerite de Navarre, and Cop eventually found refuge in Basel, Switzerland.

The second event was the point of no return with the *Affaire des Placards* in October 1534. Posters denouncing the Catholic Mass were posted publicly in several cities and on the door of François's bedchamber while he slept at Amboise. The leaders of the Sorbonne persuaded François that Protestants wanted to provoke an uprising in France. In response to the posters, an elaborate procession against the heretics was organized in January 1535, during which at least twenty heretics were burned to death and scores of others fled the city.[17] The procession advanced throughout the city with royal princes, numerous relics, and reliquary caskets including those of Saint Marcel and Saint Geneviève. The *Affaire des Placards* "marked the termination of Lutheran success in France and, despite the later Calvinist explosion, the end of any hope that the Reformation might conquer the country."[18]

As a forerunner of the French Reformation who remained within the Catholic tradition, Lefèvre has been overlooked and remains largely unknown. Yet unquestionably, "the theological position he established for himself was distinctly evangelical in character" and "Lefèvre and the Reformers were of one mind in their understanding of the fundamentals of the gospel."[19] The French poet Agrippa d'Aubigné reminds us that "the history of the Reformation shows that if one cannot make anything new with old things, and that there must be new vessels for new wine, there must also be new wine for the new vessels."[20] Lefèvre had sought to put the new wine of the gospel in the old vessel of Catholicism.

Despite his valiant efforts at reform within the Catholic Church, Lefèvre had not been able to preserve the illusion that one could evangelize in a way that called into question the order of the kingdom or threatened the king's religion. Toward the end of his life, he found refuge at Nérac with Marguerite, Queen of Navarre. He was too old to play an active role in the

17. Bost, *Histoire des protestants de France*, 44.
18. Elton, *Reformation Europe*, 80.
19. Hughes, *Lefèvre*, 97.
20. D'Aubigné, *Histoire de la Réformation*, 10.

French Reformation and died in his sleep, afflicted that he had not merited the fate of those slain for the gospel that he taught them.[21] We are told that his last words were inscribed on his tombstone: "I leave my body to the earth, my spirit to God, my possessions to the poor."[22]

21. Miquel, *Guerres de religion*, 62–63.
22. Félice, *Histoire des protestants*, 37.

Chapter 2

Guillaume Farel (1489–1565)
Defender of the Gospel

STEPHEN M. DAVIS

Guillaume (William) Farel was a key minister in the development of Reformed churches in the sixteenth century and established a network of Francophone preachers. A contemporary of Calvin and coworker with him in Geneva, he was a gifted man of contradictions and controversy that dogged him throughout his ministry. A man of action, he braved danger, escaped attackers, and survived assassination attempts to advance God's work.

Farel was twenty years Calvin's senior and one of the first Frenchmen to echo Luther's protest. Some writers have portrayed Farel as a "fiery-tempered and long-winded reforming preacher handing over the reins of his disorganized Genevan Reformation to the mighty Calvin for codification and solidification." For other historians, Farel "is in the process of 'rehabilitation'" since Calvin's "pre-eminent force in the establishment and development of Reformed thought" has been called into question.[1] Although he lived in Calvin's shadow, Farel was instrumental in Calvin's call to Geneva in 1536. He has been described as a bulldozer who destroyed a dilapidated theological building while Calvin built a new one.[2]

---

1. Zuidema and Van Raalte, *Early French Reform*, 3.
2. Zuidema, *Guillaume Farel*, 13.

Farel was born in a village near Gap in Dauphiné in 1489, into a family devoted to the Catholic faith. His early life was spent in a strict religious atmosphere. Later in life, he recalled a pilgrimage as a young man that was crucial in the process of transformation in his life. He was shown an alleged piece of Christ's cross and told that if the piece was stolen or hidden, it would miraculously return to its rightful place. This was seen as confirmation of the presence of Christ in the Catholic Church. Years later he would see another piece of the cross in Paris and was struck by the difference between the color and texture of the two pieces. Farel saw through the deception and doubts arose about Catholic teaching and traditions.[3]

On his way to Paris in 1509 or 1510, he was deeply saddened by the corruption he witnessed in the cities he traversed. Upon his arrival at the University of Paris, one of Farel's professors was Jacques Lefèvre d'Étaples, a notable French humanist who had a lasting impact on Farel. Lefèvre lectured at the Abbey of Saint-Germaine, whose superior, Guillaume Briçonnet II (1472–1534), later became the bishop in Meaux. Lefèvre began to doubt the value of Catholic religious practices and discovered that the stories of saints were based on legends rather than reality. By 1521, after careful reading of the Scriptures, Farel was convinced that the basis for Christian belief was the explicit teaching of the word of God and the grace of God freely offered in Jesus Christ. Once he embraced these truths, he knew he could no longer remain in Paris without risking the ire of the Sorbonne and renounced his place as professor at the Collège du Cardinal le Moine.[4]

Meaux became the center of evangelical activity, and Bishop Briçonnet preached clearly that any other gospel than the gospel of Christ was false.[5] He undertook a campaign to reform the Catholic Church and called Lefèvre to lead missionary efforts. Soon, however, Lefèvre and Farel found themselves at odds with the Catholic hierarchy. Farel's contestation of the veneration of Mary and the saints provoked the ire of the Faculty of Theology at the Sorbonne in Paris and drew growing hostility from parliamentarians. Lefèvre and Briçonnet agreed that reform in the Catholic Church needed to come slowly; Farel advocated an extreme reform and was considered especially dangerous because of his opposition to the dogma of purgatory.[6]

3. Zuidema, *Guillaume Farel*, 19–20.
4. Carayon, *Guillaume Farel*, 9–11.
5. Carayon, *Guillaume Farel*, 12.
6. Miquel, *Guerres de religion*, 10.

When Briçonnet was called upon to post papal bulls of Pope Clement VII, which included the announcement of new indulgences, the people of Meaux were indignant. Farel was exiled, the posters ripped down, and the pope was reviled as antichrist. Meaux entered into rebellion against the church, and the first persecution was unleashed. Briçonnet acted in vain to calm the spirits. He instructed the priests to once again read prayers for the dead, to invoke the Virgin and saints, and took the statues and images of saints under his protection.[7]

Farel left Meaux in 1522 and returned to Gap with the desire to reform his birthplace. He was not received with open arms and was soon obliged to leave the city. However, during his time there, his family members were struck by his piety. For some, it was the beginning of their journey to discover the gospel. One notable convert, Anémond de Coct, left Gap in 1523 to study under Luther at the University of Wittenberg. Farel briefly returned to Meaux before going to Paris, where his message was unwelcome. No longer able to preach in Gap, Meaux, or Paris, Farel decided to find refuge in Switzerland. Switzerland already had preachers of the Reformation when Farel arrived in 1524—Ulrich Zwingli in Zurich, Berthold Haller in Bern, and Oecolampadius in Basel.[8]

When Farel arrived in Basel, Oecolampadius was impressed by Farel's zeal and took him under his wing to discuss and defend his beliefs. Farel was forbidden by the clergy to publicly affirm new teachings and made enemies through his stubborn refusal to submit. He left Basel and passed through Strasbourg where he met Martin Bucer and Wolfgang Capiton, from whom he received the hand of fellowship. Pressed to preach the gospel, he accepted an invitation from Oecolampadius to Montbéliard, where he was well received by residents who had already been exposed to the gospel. He began making disciples and was opposed by the clergy. One day he came face to face with a procession preceded by two monks carrying a statue of Saint Anthony. Farel exploded in anger, snatched the statue from their hands, and threw it into the river. He was chased from the city and departed for Strasbourg. There he met Lefèvre, who had been forced to leave France to escape his enemies. Several days later, Farel visited Mulhouse, spent several days in Basel, and arrived in Neuchâtel, where he preached and was forced to leave the city. Toward the end of 1526, he arrived in Aigle and presented himself as a schoolteacher under the name Guillaume Ursin. He

---

7. Miquel, *Guerres de religion*, 54–58.
8. Carayon, *Guillaume Farel*, 13.

invited parents to the classes, where he explained Scripture to them. There was much consternation when he revealed his true identity. The clergy opposed him, and Catholics and Protestants almost came to violence.[9]

After traveling through other cities, Farel was forbidden to preach in Neuchâtel and settled for a cemetery provided by a priest in the village of Serrières. As he preached, soldiers came to hear him and to his surprise led him to Neuchâtel, where he found many open to the gospel. The inhabitants were so taken with the teaching that to the chagrin of the city's religious leaders, they offered him the hospital's chapel to preach. Farel defended himself before the local magistrates, who were undecided on their course of action. As his preaching spread, people began destroying images in Catholic churches. In the town of Boudevilliers, Farel entered the Catholic church, while the priest observed the Mass and his companion Antoine Boyve snatched the host from the priest's hands. The priests rang the church bells and gathered a crowd that chased Farel and Boyve from the town. They escaped, only to be seized in Valangin and spared due to the intervention of passing peasants from Neuchâtel. Farel sensed that his mission was complete in this city and left to continue his ministry elsewhere.[10]

Geneva had enjoyed a democratic form of government under the administration of bishops despite the efforts of the Duke of Savoy, Charles III, to remove secular power from the bishop and freedom from the bourgeoisie. He finally succeeded, and for five years the duke exercised his tyranny before leaving for his estates in Piedmont in 1525. Amid these struggles for control of the city, the Reformation penetrated the city. Beginning in 1528, there were protests against the immorality and ignorance of the clergy. Some of the bourgeois stopped attending Mass and ate meat on days it was forbidden. The city council responded by ordering fines or imprisonment for those who committed these infractions. These conflicts prepared Geneva to receive the gospel upon Farel's arrival in 1532, his first visit to the city. The gospel was preached to those already leaning toward evangelical teaching. He was forced to leave Geneva by the city council after complaints from local priests.[11]

Farel returned to Geneva in 1534 under the protection of the government authorities of Bern. He opened a place of worship in a church convent and deployed his energy to win members of the city council to his views.

9. Carayon, *Guillaume Farel*, 13–16.
10. Carayon, *Guillaume Farel*, 18–21.
11. Carayon, *Guillaume Farel*, 23–28.

They were reticent to publicly identify with Farel out of fear of losing the support of Catholics. However, permission was given for a public debate, and the council invited Catholic priests and theologians from Geneva and from other places to attend. Two Catholic theologians, Caroli and Chapuis, defended Catholic teaching, and after a long disputation admitted defeat. The council remained hesitant to commit its support for the Reformation. But the people rallied to Farel's teachings, and as their numbers grew, he took over other churches in the city, where people destroyed images and overturned altars. The council again invited priests to a conference to defend Catholic teaching. When they did not attend, the council abolished the Mass and declared the establishment of the Reformation in Geneva. Geneva, with the assistance of Bern, successfully foiled an attempt by the Duke of Savoy to take over the city, and a Protestant Republic rose on the ruins of feudal Geneva.[12]

In 1536, Calvin passed through Geneva, where Farel needed help in organizing a new church. Calvin first resisted but eventually yielded after Farel threatened him with the Lord's punishment. They combined their energy and genius in establishing and enforcing morality in the city. Every citizen either swore to observe the Confession of Faith or was forced to leave the city. They excommunicated the godless and the heretics, calling on secular authorities to carry out ecclesiastical laws. There was staunch resistance, and both Calvin and Farel were briefly chased from Geneva in 1538 due to the religious laws they sought to impose on the city. Farel accompanied Calvin to Bern, Zurich, and Basel before returning to Neuchâtel while Calvin went to Strasbourg. The Genevans recalled the two ministers in 1541. Calvin returned while Farel remained at Neuchâtel, where he served until his death. He continued to preach in other cities as well, often in great danger, with a brief return to France to establish a church in Grenoble and visit Gap.[13]

Calvin acknowledged his debt to Farel in the dedication to his commentary on Titus as a testament to "that holy union and friendship which exists between us."[14] Calvin compared himself to Titus and Farel to Paul. As Titus completed the work begun by Paul on the island of Crete, Calvin continued the work begun by Farel. Calvin's words are remarkable concerning Farel: "When you had made some progress in rearing this church with vast

---

12. Carayon, *Guillaume Farel*, 31–34.
13. Carayon, *Guillaume Farel*, 35–36.
14. Calvin, *Commentaries on the Epistles*, 275.

exertions, and at great risk, after some time had elapsed I came, first as your assistant, and afterwards was left as your successor, that I might endeavor to carry forward, to the best of my ability, that work which you had so well and so successfully begun."[15]

One notable chapter of persecution connected to Farel took place in the Luberon region of France against the Waldensians (*Vaudois*), the spiritual descendants of Pierre Waldo (1140–1218), which led to the Mérindol massacre in 1545. The massacre was preceded by a decisive meeting that took place in Piedmont in 1532 with Waldensian leadership from different regions. Over six days, Farel, in exile from Meaux, convinced them to preserve only two sacraments, baptism and the Eucharist, without the mystical sense given by the Catholic Church.[16] Farel welcomed them to the Reformed faith with enthusiasm and called them the elder sons of the Reformation.[17]

In 1540 Farel was warned by a courier of an order condemning nineteen Waldensians to be burned at the stake in three different places.[18] Farel contacted Swiss and German cities to intercede diplomatically with François I. The king charged the governor of Piedmont, Guillaume du Ballay, to investigate the Waldensians. When he delivered a favorable report, the king suspended the order and demanded the appearance of the Waldensian elders before the parlement within three months. On April 6, 1541, instead of sending the elders before the Parlement of Aix to renounce their faith, the Mérindoliens sent their Confession of Faith to the parlement and the king to explain their faith in Jesus Christ and the Scriptures. They were willing to submit to all laws but requested freedom to practice their faith. The king granted another three-month delay, and the parlement sent the bishop of Cavaillon to Mérindol to receive their renunciation of heresy on the spot.[19]

After further delays and the refusal to recant their faith, the king finally resolved in March 1543 to carry out the order against Mérindol. Once again, German Protestant princes, urged by Farel and Calvin, intervened with the king. In April 1544, the Waldensians presented a petition

15. Bèze, *Life of Calvin*, 16–17.

16. Baptism in the Reformed tradition was infant baptism. The Anabaptist practice of adult or believer's baptism was strongly condemned in the confessions of the sixteenth century as "strange and erroneous doctrines . . . among other damnable and depraved opinions." See Dennison, *Reformed Confessions*, 1:295.

17. Miquel, *Guerres de religion*, 121.

18. Miquel, *Guerres de religion*, 123–24.

19. Félice, *Histoire des protestants*, 61.

to the king to obtain justice against those who reproached their faith with the intent to confiscate their possessions. The king sent three members of his council and a theologian to establish whether the Waldensians were heretics. The Waldensians sensed that the king hesitated to employ force against them. Those in Geneva even thought that they had turned back the royal power.[20]

In March 1545, Paulin de La Garde, the leader of a fearsome band of roving mercenaries, received an order from the parlement to proceed to the total eradication of the heretics. Paulin marched on Mérindol as the inhabitants fled to the Luberon forests. Two hundred farms were burned and the villagers watched the devastation from a distance. Their houses were burned down, their harvests ripped from the ground, their wells filled and plugged, and their bridges destroyed. The Waldensian men mounted upward and joined their brothers in the villages of La Coste and Cabrières-du-Comtat. In the fortified village of Cabrières, they decided to stand and resist with only three hundred combatants.[21]

In the ensuing combat, the Waldensians battled courageously but were no match for the cannons of the enemy. They proposed to open the gates when safe passage was promised to Germany. With the promise received, those who left the village were immediately seized and executed in a nearby meadow. The female combatants were locked up in a barn, which was then set ablaze. In one month, nine hundred houses were burned, twenty-four villages were destroyed, and three thousand people were massacred.[22] The massacre of the Waldensians was met with indignation throughout the kingdom. The king ordered an investigation and demanded an accounting of the expedition. Calvin and Farel were devastated by the news and requested intervention from the Swiss. The king's justification to the Swiss was that the Waldensians were disloyal subjects and were punished because they refused to pay the tithe.[23]

Calvin wrote to the ministers at Neuchâtel and Farel in 1558, consternated by Farel's proposed marriage to a sixteen-year-old girl. At the age of sixty-nine, Farel may have been thinking about the care he would need for his infirmities. In his letter to Farel, Calvin reminded him that he had already refused an invitation to his marriage ceremony and was

20. Miquel, *Guerres de religion*, 124–27.
21. Félice, *Histoire des protestants*, 62–63.
22. Miquel, *Guerres de religion*, 127–33.
23. Miquel, *Guerres de religion*, 134–35.

surprised by another invitation. He considered it "inexpedient" to attend and reproached Farel for his lack of prudence in delaying the marriage and prolonging the scandal. In his letter to the ministers, Calvin recognized that "there is no law which forbids such a marriage" but feared a scandal. Yet he questioned "whether it be a suitable remedy to break off a marriage which is already contracted." Short of defending his old friend, Calvin appealed to the ministers "to remember how he has employed himself, during the space of thirty-six years and more, in serving God and edifying his church ... and even what advantages you have derived from him."[24]

Farel visited Calvin before the latter's death. After his visit, he was invited by the inhabitants of Metz to see the progress of the Reformation in their city. Upon his return to Neuchâtel, the fatigue of his voyage aggravated his infirmities. He fell ill and died September 13, 1565, at the age of seventy-six. At the beginning of his life, he was a zealous servant of the Catholic Church. Once his eyes were opened to the gospel of grace and the authority of Scripture, he became a relentless adversary of Catholicism, a fervent minister of the gospel, and a church-planting missionary. As a man of action, he might be rightly criticized for his harsh temperament and incidents of violence, for his lack of prudence and common sense. He was a lion and not a dove. Beaten, imprisoned, and chased from town to town, he lived fearlessly for the truth of God's word and upon his death entered into the joy of his Lord.[25]

---

24. Calvin, *Letters of John Calvin*, 3:473–75.
25. Carayon, *Guillaume Farel*, 39–40.

Chapter 3

Louis de Berquin (1490–1529)
Christian Martyr

MARTIN I. KLAUBER

LOUIS DE BERQUIN IS more well known for his death than his life. He was burned at the stake for espousing Lutheran ideas in 1529, in the very early days of the Reformation in France. As he approached the executioner, he tried to cry out his last words, but the cries of the nearby soldiers drowned him out. After his death, the grand *pénitencier* allegedly remarked that he had never seen someone die in a more Christian way. His books had been publicly burned just a few days before, after being accused of Lutheran tendencies at a time when the Sorbonne and the Parlement of Paris were very concerned about the influx of the so-called Lutheran heresy into France. However, Berquin fits better as a humanist who was open to ideas for reforming the church and never formally abjured his Roman Catholic faith. He belongs to a category of French humanists such as Jacques Lefèvre d'Étaples and Guillaume Briçonnet, who were advocates of the idea of *ad fontes*, or a return to sources and for making classic texts such as the Bible available in the vernacular.[1]

To some extent, Berquin was a victim of circumstances. Religious persecution had its fits and starts in the 1520s, especially in Paris. In 1528, a statue of the Virgin and the baby Jesus was mutilated. It caused such a stir

---

1. Joblin, *Louis de Berquin*, 1–2.

that François I was moved to tears. The king decided to reinstall the statue and personally participated in a grand expiatory procession. This incident indicates how iconoclasm resulted in periods of persecution and increased public abhorrence of the new Lutheran ideas infiltrating the realm.[2]

Berquin was born in the town of Passy, then just outside of Paris, around 1490. His family had owned land in the small town of Vieux-Berquin in Flanders, which Berquin inherited. His father also owned land in the town of Cormeilles, north of Paris. The list of property confiscated from him after his death indicates his family possessed some wealth, but he never married.[3] So, he was able to afford to pursue his academic interests. He studied at the famous law faculty at Orléans, starting in 1506 or 1507, and received a solid education in the humanist method. The humanist Jérôme Aléandre may have been one of his instructors, and he met a fellow student, Nicole Bérault, who would help lead him on the path toward a more evangelical faith. Bérault had previously studied in Italy under Aléandre and became a professor of poetry and law. He then studied at Orléans under Erasmus and maintained a lifelong correspondence with the prince of the humanists. He was licensed in law in 1511 and was a guardian for students who lived in his home, including the humanists Melchior Wolmar and Etienne Dolet.

Bérault moved to Paris in 1512, where he taught courses on Cicero, Suetonius, Aristotle, and Politian. According to Alain Joblin, Bérault displayed "a very open spirit, curiosity, and philosophical and religious tolerance. He distinguished himself, especially by a virulent condemnation of scholasticism, which caused quite a bit of trouble with the Sorbonne starting in 1524." He translated classical works and corresponded with Guillaume Budé, Erasmus, and the printer Josse Badius. In 1530, he became a professor of Greek at the newly formed Collège des Trois Langues. He was well connected and protected by men in high positions such as the cardinal, Odet de Coligny, and even King François I. Bérault was a good person for Berquin to know, and their friendship opened doors for Berquin to pursue his scholarly interests.[4]

When Berquin came to Paris, he benefitted from these introductions. He became friends with men of culture and high rank such as François de

---

2. Joblin, *Louis de Berquin*, 2–3.

3. On Berquin's early life see Beuzart, "Sur l'origine de Louis de Berquin," 45–49.

4. For more on Bérault, see Galand-Hallyn, "*Praelectio in Suetonium* de Nicholas Bérault," 62–93.

Loynes of the Parlement of Paris; Claude Braché, treasurer for the king; and Louis Ruzé, lieutenant of the provost of Paris and also son of the chancellor of the University of Orléans. François de Loynes, in turn, was friends with Guillaume Budé, and his daughter Antoinette was an accomplished poet. Her Parisian salon was frequented by other famous poets such as Pierre de Ronsard and Joachim du Bellay. Ruzé was friendly with the eminent French printer Josse Bade. These crucial contacts helped Berquin begin an epistolary relationship with the great Erasmus. Historian Barthélemy Hauréau claims that Berquin came to love Erasmus as a father and, according to Berquin, Erasmus loved him as a son.[5]

Berquin worked with Bérault's early publications, which translated classical and humanist texts. For example, they worked on translating the works of the Italian humanist Angelo Poliziano (1454–94); Lucian, whose second-century works were written in Greek; and the first-century author Pliny's works on natural history. Lucian, in particular, was an expert in the art of rhetoric, and Berquin translated his *Éloge de la mouche* in 1517. This work covered important topics such as the immortality of the soul and was critical, in a humorous way, of the moral vices of the time. It was an example of a work that focused on simplicity and clarity, designed to reach a wider audience.[6]

In working on these translations, Berquin attempted to make some of the great texts available in French to ensure a wider audience. He rejected aspects of medieval scholastic writing and attempted to use the *ad fontes* method to create the best texts in their historical and philological context.

Berquin ran into trouble in his relationship with Erasmus when he translated some of his works into French, particularly Erasmus's *Encomium matrimonis*. Berquin omitted the question mark in his translation and made it seem like Erasmus was questioning the biblical basis of clerical celibacy. This was a dangerous accusation, as one of the significant differences between the early Lutheran movement and Roman Catholicism had to do with the celibacy of the priesthood. Making Erasmus seem to support the Protestant position was dangerous to Erasmus, who was very careful in the limits he put on his criticism of the church.[7]

As early as 1523, Roman Catholic authorities began to be concerned about Berquin's orthodoxy. He had defended Jacques Lefèvre d'Étaple's

---

5. Hauréau, "Louis de Berquin," 456.
6. Joblin, *Louis de Berquin*, 26.
7. Joblin, *Louis de Berquin*, 28–29.

vernacular translation of the Gospels against attacks from the Sorbonne. This was the same timeframe that Jean Vallières had publicly criticized the virgin birth of Christ, and his punishment was having his tongue cut off. Noël Bedier (or Béda), a Doctor of Theology at Paris (c. 1470–1535) and a noted opponent of the new humanist method of studies, led the charge against Berquin. Part of the condemnation was that he was not a trained theologian and, therefore, was unqualified to make such statements. As the protector of orthodoxy, the Sorbonne tried to rid the realm of any suspicious Lutheran ideas rapidly infiltrating France.

Furthermore, the king had just ordered Luther's books to be burned in April 1523. Berquin's home was searched, and the authorities rummaged through his library and papers. They found books written by Luther, Melanchthon, and Karlstadt and the satirical treatment of Pope Julius II, *Julius Excluded from Heaven* (1514), attributed to Erasmus. Later in 1523 the theologians condemned works by Luther, Melanchthon, and Erasmus. After a failed examination by the Faculty of Theology in Paris, his case was referred to the Parlement of Paris, and he was imprisoned. Then François I intervened and demanded that the case be referred to his private council, and Berquin was allowed to recant any heterodox views to secure his release.[8]

However, Berquin's fortunes would soon change when François I, captured by the emperor's forces at the Battle of Pavia (1525), was held prisoner in Spain. With the king absent from court, the Queen Regent, Louise de Savoie, stepped up efforts to repress heresy, and three of Erasmus's works were censured. Berquin was arrested again on January 24, 1526. One of the problems for Berquin is that some of his books contained marginal notes where he expressed support for some Lutheran ideas. They also found a work that he had allegedly written, *La farce des théologastres* (*The Farce of the Bad Theologians*). It was a typical humanist comedy that ridiculed the scholasticism of the Sorbonne for its sterile discourses on minor topics that did not lead to personal piety. The characters in the work included the Theologian and the Friar, who represented the censors' established beliefs. The character called Faith was struggling with an illness caused by these sophists, who emphasized the minute specifics of doctrine. The lack of religious security made the character suffer from a colic called sophistic passion. The heroes of the story were the characters Scripture and Reason.

---

8. Garside, "Farce des Theologastres," 47–48; Weiss, "Louis de Berquin," 180–81. Peña, "French 'Confessionalization,'" 14–15.

Scripture was all beat up and dirty, with all the marginal glosses in the margins that seemed to have a superiority of authority to the extent that the text itself was lost. Once Scripture is physically cleansed from these accretions and can be read by the character Faith, the disease can be cured. Berquin himself appeared in the work as a character from Germany called Mercury, who pointed Faith to the pure Word of God.[9] This work seemed to support the Lutheran idea of *sola scriptura* and aroused the suspicion of religious authorities at the Sorbonne. Although Berquin did not affirm that he was a Lutheran, he was sympathetic to some of his ideas and supported the idea that the church needed to be reformed.[10]

In addition, his books and papers were publicly burned. Finally, he was commanded not to write any more on theological matters since he had insufficient training. He was accused of supporting the ideas of justification by faith, praying to God in the vernacular, and mistranslating the Apostles' Creed. Forty of Berquin's propositions were declared heterodox, but he defended himself by saying that they were taken from Erasmus, and he was not a declared heretic. Erasmus had written a letter to Béda dated June 15, 1525, saying he had never met Berquin personally. Furthermore, Erasmus argued that one should look to the original Latin works rather than translations. After all, Berquin could have added virtually anything he wanted. Erasmus said he did not even know that Berquin was translating some of his works. In March 1526, Erasmus sent a letter to Béda, again saying that Berquin had taken extracts from his works and added his ideas to them.[11]

Then, Marguerite d'Angoulême, Queen of Navarre and sister of the king, wrote to her brother and asked him to order Berquin's release. Marguerite had some degree of sympathy for these early humanists, who seemed to espouse some evangelical ideas. The king wrote demanding that no action be taken against Berquin without his consent. However, parlement ignored the king's command and ordered Berquin's remaining books to be burned. Again, François I came to his rescue when he returned in March of 1526, and he was concerned that the parlement was going too far in prosecuting scholars such as Jacques Lefèvre d'Etaples. However, the parlement delayed the release of Berquin until November 1526, when the king sent the provost to have him forcibly released.[12] Berquin then ignored

9. Garside, "Farce des Theologastres," 45–82.
10. Joblin, *Louis de Berquin*, 64–65.
11. Mann, "Louis de Berquin," 310.
12. Peña, "French 'Confessionalization,'" 15–16.

Erasmus's advice to be more careful. He demanded that the charges against him be expunged and publicly criticized Béda. In Berquin's translation of Erasmus's *Enchiridion* in 1526, he inserted passages from Luther and William Farel to make it seem like Erasmus was endorsing their ideas. Erasmus was disappointed and defended himself by saying that Berquin had again mistranslated his work.[13]

On April 15, 1529, Berquin was arrested again. The problem was that this was the third arrest, and the punishments were more severe for repeat offenders. Berquin refused to recant his alleged errors and was quickly sentenced to life in prison. Two days later, after being forced to perform a public act of penance in Notre Dame Cathedral, he was strangled by the executioner before his body was burned at the stake at the Place de Grève in front of a large crowd. This time, the king did not intervene on his behalf. Erasmus commented that he died with courage and dignity. Allegedly, John Calvin was present to witness the execution, and many were impressed with Berquin's bravery and steadfastness. The French poet Clément Marot composed a poem in his honor, "Sur le martyr de Berquin." Erasmus said that he was sure that Berquin died defending his faith but noted that it was sometimes difficult to distinguish between errors and heresies. According to Théodore de Bèze, "Berquin would have been a second Luther had he found in François I a second elector." Bèze also commented, "No man died as a better Christian than Berquin."[14] Although this was clearly an overstatement of Berquin's abilities, it shows how important governmental protection was for some of these early reformers.

---

13. Joblin, *Louis de Berquin*, 31.
14. Bèze, *Histoire ecclésiastique*, 8.

Chapter 4

Marguerite de Navarre (1492–1549)
Guardian Angel

STEPHEN M. DAVIS

QUEEN MARGUERITE DE NAVARRE was the sister of King Francois I, mother of Huguenot Queen Jeanne d'Albret, and grandmother of Henri IV (r. 1589–1610).[1] Under the influence of the Christian humanism of Erasmus, she supported reform efforts in her beloved Catholic Church. She belonged to that group of Catholics influenced by the Renaissance who embraced Reformation teachings yet remained loyal to the Catholic Church. Unlike her daughter, she never identified herself as Reformed, although she paved the way for Jeanne, who converted to Protestantism in 1560.

Throughout church history, God placed women in positions of influence to advance his work. Marguerite worked to renew the Catholic Church from within in the latter years of the Renaissance and early years of the Protestant Reformation in France. It has been argued that she "held an anomalous position in France because of her unique political status, and that she operated in both traditional 'female' and traditional 'male' roles."[2] In addition to her political influence, at a time when most women

---

1. Also known as Marguerite de France, Marguerite d'Alençon, and Marguerite d'Angoulême. She should be distinguished from Marguerite de Valois, Duchess of Berry (1523–74), and from Marguerite de Valois (1553–1615), known also as La Reine Margot, the first wife of Henri IV.

2. Stephenson, *Power and Patronage*, 2.

were not taken seriously, she was "biblically literate, and respected for her theological erudition by Pope Paul III as well as by other church leaders."[3] Marguerite "could carry on a lively correspondence with the Pope while sheltering Huguenot writers and thinkers like Clément Marot."[4] By force of personality and charisma, she succeeded in a man's world, although her gender disqualified her from the throne. In the literary world, she is known for her great Renaissance work *Heptaméron*, a collection of seventy-two tales told by five women and five men stranded in an abbey. The stories about love affairs "could have been documented by the author from contemporary life."[5]

Marguerite's parents were Charles d'Orléans, Count of Angoulême (1459–96), and Louise de Savoie (1476–1531). When the kings of France, Charles VIII and Louis XII, died without male heirs, the Angoulême branch of the Valois was next in line to the throne. Marguerite's brother François I was the first in the Angoulême-Valois line of French kings that lasted until Henri III's assassination in 1589, followed by the Bourbon dynasty under Henri IV. Marguerite's mother "saw to it that her daughter was educated alongside François in French, Spanish, English, Hebrew, Latin, and some Italian and German, as well as philosophy, theology, literature, and history."[6]

When François I ascended to the throne after the death of Louis XII in 1515, Marguerite created a royal court that welcomed writers and artists. In 1517 her brother made her Duchess of Berry and "elevated the duchy to a *duché-pairie*, or ducal peerage." Her position has been described as an "honorary male" and "one of the very few female peers of the realm in France."[7] She was acquainted with the works of Erasmus, the Renaissance humanist, and the Reformation writings of Martin Luther and John Calvin. Marguerite discreetly supported the Reformers and their teachings and was active with the reform movement within the Catholic Church at Meaux under Bishop Guillaume Briçonnet and Jacques Lefèvre d'Étaples.[8]

Marguerite figured as the guardian angel of the evangelicals during the first half of the sixteenth century. There was initially little resistance from the monarchy toward the new teachings until Protestantism became

3. Thysell, *Pleasure of Discernment*, 5.
4. Shumaker, "Refuge, Resistance, and Rebellion," 3.
5. Barzun, *From Dawn to Decadence*, 87.
6. Thysell, *Pleasure of Discernment*, 6.
7. Stephenson, *Power and Patronage*, 3–4.
8. Bayrou, *Henri IV*, 37–39.

perceived as a threat to existing power structures. Marguerite corresponded with Bishop Briçonnet beginning in 1521 and maintained that her brother François and her mother Louise de Savoie were eager to know God's truth. Lefèvre wrote to Farel that François had removed obstacles to reading the New Testament every Sunday and holidays. Despite impediments from the Faculty of Theology, and under royal protection by Marguerite, the writings of Lefèvre were widely diffused.[9]

From all appearances, Marguerite discovered the teaching of justification by faith and experienced a genuine religious conversion. Her writings and her poetry testify to her spiritual sensitivity accompanied by her charitable works. Her poetry shows the influence of Calvin and alludes to the elect in *Le triomphe de l'Agneau: Or, il a donc prédestiné les siens; Pour leur donner à jouir de ses biens.* (*The Triumph of the Lamb: Now, he has predestinated his own; To give them the enjoyment of his possessions*). Even when attacked by the Sorbonne, she guarded the hope of a reform wrought at the interior of the church. At this stage, Luther was hardly known in France, even if the events of 1517 at Wittenberg and Luther's excommunication had been communicated by travelers.[10] She was involved with the translation of some of Martin Luther's writings into French, supported Bishop Briçonnet's opposition to the sale of indulgences and the veneration of saints' relics, and "saved Jacques Lefèvre, the translator into French of the New Testament, from execution after his condemnation by the Sorbonne."[11]

Marguerite's husbands did not share her religious interests. Her first marriage in 1509 was with Charles, Duke of Alençon, a political marriage under the auspices of Louis XII between the houses of Alençon and Angoulême. Charles died in 1525, two months after the catastrophic Battle of Pavia, during which François I and Henri d'Albret, King of Navarre, were taken prisoner by Holy Roman Emperor Charles V (1500–1558). Henri escaped from prison, and Marguerite negotiated the release of François, leading to the Treaty of Madrid in January 1526. When her brother gave her hand in marriage to Henri d'Albret, she became queen of the semi-sovereign state of Navarre and established courts at Pau and Nérac. The marriage was politically advantageous for François, Henri, and Marguerite in the expansion of territories. François allied himself with the powerful House of Foix-Navarre-Albret, and Henri hoped to recover the southern portion

---

9. Miquel, *Guerres de religion*, 51.
10. Miquel, *Guerres de religion*, 52.
11. Stjerna, *Women and the Reformation*, 152.

of Navarre on the border of Spain, lost to the Habsburgs. François was not prepared to go to war with Spain over Spanish Navarre, and the unresolved territorial problem was passed on to Marguerite's daughter Jeanne.[12]

Marguerite gave birth to Jeanne d'Albret in 1528, a year after her marriage to Henri. Their only son, Jean, died in 1530 at six months old. After the death of her son and then her mother in 1531, Marguerite wrote *Miroir de l'âme pécheresse* (*Mirror of the Sinful Soul*) to reflect her misery and journey of faith in her pursuit of Christ. After the Faculty of Theology at Paris condemned the poem in 1533 for its Lutheran ideas, she established herself at Nérac, which became a refuge for those persecuted by the Catholic Church. There she was accompanied by her chaplain Gérald Roussel, Bishop of Oloran, who was charged with heresy by the Parlement of Paris after his sermons scandalized the French court. John Calvin, Clément Marot, and Lefèvre d'Étaples found refuge there as well. Nicolas Cop, rector of the Sorbonne, was forced to flee Paris for Nérac in 1533 after his evangelical sermon on All Saints' Day before going to Switzerland. Calvin fled with him and encountered Lefèvre in Nérac. Under their influence, the surrounding cities of Sainte-Foy-la Grande, Bergerac, Agen, Clairac, and finally La Rochelle were soon won over to the Reformed faith. Yet little by little, royal opinion was hardened toward those who became known as Huguenots.[13]

François I protected Marguerite and those who found refuge with her until the *Affaire des Placards* in October 1534. Marguerite was clearly appalled and had never condoned smashing images or other radical actions. Yet some Catholics blamed her for the incident. She left the court and from that moment on François I consented to brutal measures to suppress the heretics with widespread persecution.[14] Calvin had nurtured high hopes for her influence and was concerned about compromises made by French Huguenots under persecution. Marguerite "continued to outwardly observe Catholic religious practices to Calvin's dismay."[15] She was "particularly drawn to mysticism [and] envisioned Church reform to unfold from the spiritual renewal of individuals."[16]

Although Marguerite adopted much of the substance of Reformation teachings, she could not conceive of a new church and a new faith. Her

---

12. Babelon, *Henri IV*, 28.
13. Babelon, *Henri IV*, 76.
14. Félice, *Histoire des protestants*, 45.
15. Stjerna, *Women and the Reformation*, 153.
16. Stjerna, *Women and the Reformation*, 152.

"goals and ambitions for reform were not fulfilled . . . [yet] for more than forty years Marguerite de Navarre occupied a position of great power in early sixteenth-century France."[17] Her courage in the support of humanists and Huguenots and her influence with her brother to prevent the arrests and execution of religious dissenters reveal the transformation she underwent. Marguerite remained a Catholic until her death in December 1549. She was one of the most remarkable figures of the early 1500s and is remembered for her contribution to the French Protestant Reformation, her advocacy for religious freedom, and her literary achievements.

---

17. Stephenson, *Power and Patronage*, 8.

Chapter 5

Michel de L'Hôpital (c. 1505–73)
Catholic Peacemaker

STEPHEN M. DAVIS

MICHEL DE L'HÔPITAL (ALSO known as L'Hospital) was a French statesman who served during the reigns of four kings: François I, Henri II, François II, and Charles IX. At a time when "one king, one law, one faith" was the almost unanimous opinion of the French people, L'Hôpital perceived the necessity of the separation of the state and church to free France from unending religious conflicts. Although he never converted to the Reformed religion, he worked tirelessly for peace between competing confessions. He considered freedom of conscience as the first condition of social peace.[1]

Michel de L'Hôpital was born in 1505 or 1506 in the small town of Aigueperse in Auvergne. His father Jean was attached to the service of Charles de Bourbon, Constable of France,[2] and sent Michel to Toulouse for his studies. He only spent two years there, but the atmosphere of violence influenced what became a lifelong commitment to oppose all forms of intolerance, especially when the news spread to Toulouse of the first martyrs of French Protestantism, Jean Leclerc in Meaux (1523) and Jacques Pavanne, burned at the stake in Paris (1524).[3]

---

1. Babelon, *Henri IV*, 445.
2. The Constable of France (*Connétable*) was commander-in-chief of the king's troops.
3. Amphoux, *Michel de L'Hôpital*, 25.

During this time the fortunes of Michel's father Jean were reversed by the troubles of Charles de Bourbon, viewed as a rival by King François I (r. 1515–47), and who was accused of a treasonous alliance with Emperor Charles V. Jean was considered Charles de Bourbon's accomplice, leading to the confiscation of his property and possessions. Michel was arrested at Toulouse and imprisoned for a brief time. Once released, without being charged with a crime, he left for Italy to join his father in Milan, which was under siege by François I. Michel left the city in disguise at the wish of his father and passed through the French army to establish himself at Padua, where he excelled in his religious studies.

Charles de Bourbon was killed during the siege of Rome in 1527, and Jean lost everything at his patron's death. Jean and Michel went to Rome, where Cardinal de Grammont persuaded both father and son to return to France. At the cardinal's death in 1534, Michel was left in Paris without protection. His father was unable to regain possession of his lands and left for Lorraine where he died. In 1537, Michel married the daughter of the *lieutenant-criminel*[4] of the Châtelet, Marie Morin, with whom he had three daughters, and became a councillor in parlement as part of the dowry.[5] Of his three daughters, only one was still alive in 1543. The loss of his two other daughters led him and his wife to contemplate the Holy Scriptures for encouragement. Their sorrow was assuaged by embracing the assurance of salvation and the prospect of seeing their daughters again in the Lord's presence.[6]

François Olivier (c. 1487–1560), Chancellor of France, recognized L'Hôpital's qualities and entrusted to him matters of significant importance. In 1542, 1546, and 1547, he was sent to preside over special judicial sessions in the cities of Riom and Tours. His work in parlement gave L'Hôpital insight into the moral condition of France and stirred in him the desire to work toward reform in eliminating abuses. He failed to advance his career where he might have had more influence to bring about changes in social, religious, and political institutions. His influential friends at the court could not persuade an appointment from François I, who saw in L'Hôpital the son of a man who had allied himself with the treasonous Charles de Bourbon. In 1544, L'Hôpital appealed to the Bishop of Mâcon, Pierre Castellan, administrator of the royal library, to intercede on his behalf to the king. But the king, gravely ill from the disease that would take his life and

---

4. The *lieutenant-criminel* was a high court official.
5. Pouilly, *Vie de Michel de L'Hôpital*, 3–14.
6. Amphoux, *Michel de L'Hôpital*, 70–75.

irritated by his failures at the hands of Henry VIII of England (r. 1509–47) and Holy Roman Emperor Charles V (r. 1519–56), failed to act on Castellan's request.[7]

On March 31, 1547, King François I died and left the crown to his son Henri II, who appointed L'Hôpital ambassador to the Council of Trent. This mission provided him the opportunity to assess ecclesiastical questions and church and state relations. The new religious ideas of Luther and Calvin had spread throughout Europe, and despite the Catholic Church's anathemas and persecution, there was the hope that religious unity could be reestablished. Pope Paul III had promised an ecumenical council in 1535, delayed it as long as possible, and named two of his teenage grandchildren cardinals to ensure that the council would be beholden to him. In 1542, he restored the institution of a supreme tribunal of inquisition charged to judge and condemn heretics. The Council of Trent was unable to meet until 1545 because of a rupture between Charles V and François I. However, the church refused any contestation of its doctrine or dogmas.

L'Hôpital was astonished at the small number of prelates in attendance and disillusioned when the high dignitaries of the church, consulted by sovereigns on the best way to achieve religious harmony, spoke with a voice contrary to the gospel and served their nation's ambitions and personal interests.[8] After his return to France, L'Hôpital was appointed Chancellor of the Duchy of Berry, a region ruled by Marguerite de Navarre, sister of François I. L'Hôpital considered that the years he administered the duchy were among his happiest. Although he conserved his title of councillor in parlement, he was mostly exempt from participation in the affairs of litigation. It was here that his desire was strengthened for the development of the social order and respect for personal convictions.[9]

As his influence grew, L'Hôpital was entrusted by the French Court with important matters of state. After the Treaty of Cateau-Cambrésis ended the Italian Wars in April 1559, he accompanied Marguerite de Valois, Duchess de Berry and daughter of François I, to sign the marriage contract with Duke Emanuele Filiberto, Charles V's nephew.[10] L'Hôpital's nomination as Chancellor of France was prompted by the violence and executions that followed the failed Conspiracy of Amboise to kidnap King François

---

7. Amphoux, *Michel de L'Hôpital*, 75–80.
8. Amphoux, *Michel de L'Hôpital*, 84–89.
9. Amphoux, *Michel de L'Hôpital*, 99–101.
10. Galand-Willemen and Petris, *Michel de L'Hospital*, 19–20.

II of France (r. 1559–60) in March 1560. The conspiracy was the work of Huguenots and other malcontents who sought to remove the king from the influence of the House of Guise that had mobilized persecution against Protestants. The conspirators sought to obtain freedom of worship and the convocation of the Estates-General to establish peace in the kingdom.

With the plot unmasked, the Duke of Guise succeeded in consolidating his power and was appointed *lieutenant-général* of the kingdom.[11] Under the duke's authority, the ringleader of the conspiracy, Jean du Barry, seigneur de la Renaudie, was killed in the Château-Renault forest four days after the failed plot. Barry's body was taken to Amboise, hung on the gallows, and then cut into five pieces exhibited at the gates of the city. His co-conspirators were hunted down and massacred without due process, their bodies hung like grape clusters from the windows of the château. The Queen Mother, Catherine de Medici (1519–89), was shocked by the savagery of the reprisals against the conspirators and realized that the unity of the kingdom was threatened. The current chancellor, François Olivier, shocked by the massacres, died of shame and sorrow several days later. Upon the visit of the Cardinal de Lorraine at his deathbed, Olivier reportedly cried, "Ah, cardinal, you damn us all!"[12] Catherine wanted a moderate in government as an advocate for reconciliation and suggested that the king appoint L'Hôpital. He became Chancellor of France on May 6, 1560, and remained in this position until September 27, 1568. Upon his appointment as chancellor, he supported the Queen Mother in seeking to counterbalance the power of the Guises.[13]

The Colloquy of Poissy in 1561 under the direction of Chancellor L'Hôpital presented the last opportunity for Catholics and Reformed believers to achieve religious tolerance and national unity in France. The chancellor had already affirmed at the Estates-General in 1560 that he desired to relegate the terms "Huguenots," "Papists," and "Lutherans" to the past and only conserve the name "Christian." In his address, he stated that conscience cannot be constrained and that constrained faith is no longer faith. The outcome of the colloquy demonstrated the incompatibility of the two faiths in reconciling, particularly on the issue of the Eucharist.[14]

---

11. The *lieutenant-général* acted on the king's behalf especially in times of crisis (*Nouveau Petit Robert*, 1456).
12. Amphoux, *Michel de L'Hôpital* 128–30.
13. Galand-Willemen and Petris, *Michel de L'Hospital*, 9.
14. Cottret, *Histoire de la Réforme Protestante*, 183.

L'Hôpital, supported by Théodore de Bèze (1519–1605), prepared the Edict of January in 1562 under Catherine de Medici, which authorized Reformed worship for the first time under certain conditions.[15] The edict offered a ray of hope to the brewing religious tension in France, even if the Parlement of Paris refused to register it immediately. The massacre of Huguenots at Vassy and Toulouse and the destruction of churches in Vendôme and Meaux aggravated religious tensions, and war became inevitable. The chancellor, fearing for his life, pretended to be ill and remained away from the court, prompting the king to send Swiss guards to protect him from Parisian Catholics. Although he attended Mass regularly, his enemies accused him of masking his real beliefs. The papal nuncio and the ambassador of Spain pressured the court to replace him with someone more clearly on their side, and L'Hôpital wrote to the pope to affirm his Catholic faith and desire for reform.[16]

During the first half of the sixteenth century, Christian humanists reflected on how religious poetry might best convey their evangelical values and Renaissance poets were looking for greater simplicity in translating the Christian faith placed at the center of human existence. L'Hôpital reimagined poetry in the light of moderate evangelical commitments from a life and vision profoundly marked by the Christian faith. His writings included literature, politics, and poetry as well as law, revealing his commitments, hopes, and failures and became a strategic means of disseminating his convictions among diverse social circles.[17] The emphasis on poetic simplicity resonated with the contemporary poetic reflections of Reformed believers whose beliefs and art were characterized by simplicity.[18] In contrast to Reformed poetry, L'Hôpital's silence on the Psalms has been interpreted as the desire to stand out from the Reformation. Some have seen his poetry as a Catholic response based on a new poetic model using evangelical language rather than the psalmic language.[19]

His masterpiece *Carmina*[20] was written from 1543 to 1573 and expressed the contradictions of his time in the struggle for religious

---

15. Babelon, *Henri IV*, 94.
16. Galand-Willemen and Petris, *Michel de L'Hospital*, 37–38.
17. Galand-Willemen and Petris, *Michel de L'Hospital*, 15–16.
18. Galand-Willemen and Petris, *Michel de L'Hospital*, 137–38.
19. Galand-Willemen and Petris, *Michel de L'Hospital*, 146–47.
20. An analysis of *Carmina* goes far beyond the objective of this brief biography. See http://www.unine.ch/micheldelhospital for the Latin text and a critical edition of *Carmena*.

reconciliation and justice. There are reflections on himself, society, human existence, and humankind's destiny.[21] The epistles trace his political fortunes as a figure of ethical and moral authority with political, moral, and literary reflections. Through classical verse, he addressed prelates, jurists, parliamentarians, and Marguerite de France, Duchess of Savoy. He drew lessons from current political and military events—France's defeat at Saint-Quentin, and the recapture of Calais and Thionville from the English.[22] Other poems develop ethical and evangelical reflections addressed to the powerful, meditations on the dangers of self-love and ignorance, considerations on luxury and greed, and exhortations on the Christian life and moderation.

L'Hôpital waged combat against the disdain of God amid political corruption and religious intolerance. Amphoux called him the "true precursor and zealous apostle of the freedom of conscience, for no one before him seems to have understood that the recognition of this freedom is the first condition of social peace."[23] He was a man of stoic wisdom living during a time of woe who sought the reconciliation of men with God. If his views had been adopted by the monarchs of France, the nation might have been spared the Wars of Religion that raged for two centuries.[24]

As Chancellor of France under Charles IX, L'Hôpital sought to neutralize and reconcile the hostility between the Catholic League and the Huguenots by affirming the necessity of religious tolerance. His attempts at national reconciliation ultimately failed, and he resigned from his position. The complexity of his thought has led historians to describe him as a crypto-Protestant, freethinker, or Christian rationalist. Perhaps the eighteenth-century biographer Louis-Jean Levesque de Pouilly best summarizes the life of the chancellor and poet. L'Hôpital was "one of the most esteemed persons that France produced, for whom the public good was always the object of his ambitions. L'Hôpital desired to make his fellow citizens happier by making them more reasonable."[25]

21. Galand-Willemen and Petris, *Michel de L'Hospital*, 79–81.
22. Galand-Willemen and Petris, *Michel de L'Hospital*, 46.
23. Amphoux, *Michel de L'Hôpital*, 3.
24. Crouzet, *Sagesse et le malheur*, 16.
25. Pouilly, *Vie de Michel de L'Hôpital*, 1.

Chapter 6

John Calvin (1509–64)
Reformed Theologian

MARTIN I. KLAUBER

John Calvin was the preeminent French Reformed theologian whose work helped to set the stage for the development of Reformed theology and church practice. Born Jean Cauvin on July 10, 1509, in Noyon, a town situated approximately sixty miles north of Paris in the Picardy region, he was the second child of Gérard Cauvin, a local notary, and Jeanne LeFranc, a devout woman. He had an older brother, Charles, and two younger brothers, Antoine and François, the latter of whom did not survive to adulthood. The death of Jeanne when Calvin was merely six years old profoundly impacted his early life, leading to his father's remarriage and the birth of two daughters. Gérard Cauvin held the position of administrative secretary to the local bishop, Charles de Hangest, which allowed Calvin to grow up in a more cultured environment influenced by the cathedral town. Following the death of his mother, Calvin was sent to reside with the de Hangest family, where he began his formal education at the Collège de Capettes. He studied alongside the sons of relatives of the de Hangest family, the Montmorts, before continuing his academic pursuits at the University of Paris.[1]

Initially, he attended the Collège de la Marche, where he studied Latin under the guidance of Mathurin Cordier. This relationship fostered

---

1. Gordon, *Calvin*, 3–5.

a lasting friendship, leading Calvin to invite Cordier to Geneva in 1536, ultimately offering him a position at the newly established Academy of Geneva in 1559. Subsequently, Calvin transferred to the Collège de Montaigu in Paris, where he was exposed to the scholastic method of teaching and theological study. While it is not definitively established, it is plausible that he studied under the eminent scholar John Major, a prominent scholastic philosopher associated with the Ockhamist tradition. By the age of 18, in 1528, Calvin had attained his Master of Arts degree, marking a significant accomplishment in his early academic career.[2]

In 1527, Gérard Calvin received yet another benefice from the lands associated with Saint-Martin-de-Martheville near Noyon, yet he directed his son, John Calvin, to pursue the study of law. The reason for the change in his course of study may have stemmed from Gérard's involvement in a property dispute with the cathedral chapter, which ultimately resulted in his excommunication in 1531. In 1528, Calvin began his legal studies at the prestigious University of Orléans. During his studies there, he encountered several people with Lutheran persuasion, which may have influenced his theological perspectives.[3]

In 1529, Calvin transferred to the University of Bourges, where he studied under the esteemed Roman law expert Andrea Alciati. At Bourges, he met Melchior Wolmar, a German humanist who taught him to read the New Testament in Greek and may have helped steer Calvin toward Lutheran theology. After approximately eighteen months at Bourges, Calvin returned to Orléans to complete his law degree. Ironically, Wolmar had also relocated to Orleans for a new position during this time. Calvin completed his legal studies in January 1531 but chose not to pursue a career as a lawyer, instead electing to follow his true academic passion for the arts, a decision made possible by the newfound freedom stemming from his father's death.[4]

Calvin subsequently relocated to Paris to pursue advanced studies in the arts at the Collège Royal, an institution that would later evolve into the esteemed Collège de France, known for its strong humanist traditions exemplified by scholars such as Jacques Lefèvre d'Étaples. Humanist intellectuals, including the prominent rector Guillaume de Budé, prioritized the examination of complete texts in their original languages, aiming to

---

2. Ganoczy, *Young Calvin*, 58–63.
3. Ganoczy, *Young Calvin*, 63–69.
4. Ganoczy, *Young Calvin*, 69–72.

achieve a more nuanced understanding of their original meanings. In the area of biblical studies, humanists favored going back to the Greek and Hebrew rather than relying solely on the Latin Vulgate. So Calvin focused on biblical texts in the original languages and the works of classical antiquity, especially authors who were noted as rhetoricians.

At this juncture, Calvin's primary scholarly endeavor was the composition of a commentary on Seneca's *De Clementia*, a project he completed in April 1532, publishing it at his own expense. Seneca, who served under Nero and was known for his rhetorical prowess in the Ciceronian tradition, authored the treatise to advocate for a measure of tolerance during Nero's reign. Calvin may have selected this work as a plea for the consideration of François I regarding the persecution of Protestants in France. Calvin displayed brilliance in Latin style and hoped that his skills in editing Seneca's work would even impress the great Erasmus. His commentary is notably ten times longer than the original text. The choice of Seneca is significant, for Calvin became enamored with Latin rhetorical style. Furthermore, the work reflects his intent to critique the excesses of tyrannical rule. Unfortunately for Calvin, the commentary failed to gain significant traction, despite his efforts to share a copy with the eminent Erasmus, leading to its limited readership and poor sales.[5]

Within eighteen months of the publication of this document, John Calvin underwent a significant shift in his religious convictions, converting to Protestantism and subsequently finding himself in a precarious position, forced to flee for his life. While precisely dating Calvin's conversion poses a challenge, it is evident that by October 1533, he had adopted a stance that placed him in considerable danger. During this period, he established a friendship with Nicholas Cop, the newly appointed rector of the University of Paris, who, with Calvin's backing, disciplined students for their participation in a theatrical performance that critiqued the evangelical Marguerite de Navarre. On All Saints' Day, 1533, Cop delivered his inaugural address, which is believed to have been penned, at least in part, by Calvin. In this discourse, Cop extolled the value of the sciences. However, he asserted that their significance diminishes in comparison to the doctrine of divine grace as the sole means of redemption from sin. As a result of this pronouncement, Cop was summoned before the parlement and subsequently fled to Basel to evade persecution.

5. Parker, *Calvin*, 37–47.

In contrast, Calvin initially returned to his hometown of Noyon, where he resigned his ecclesiastical benefices—a clear indication of his conversion. Following this, he accepted an invitation to Angoulême in southwestern France from a friend, Louis de Tillet. During his time in concealment, he utilized his father's extensive library to delve into theological studies and commenced the foundational work, the *Institutes of the Christian Religion*. He later described his move away from the Roman Catholic Church:

> When lo, a very different form of doctrine started up, not one which led us away from the Christian profession, but one which brought it back to its fountainhead, and, as it were, clearing away the dross, restored it to its original purity. Offended by the novelty, I lent an unwilling ear, and at first, I confess, strenuously and passionately resisted; for (such is the firmness or effrontery with which it is natural to men to persist in the course which they have once undertaken) it was with the greatest difficulty I was induced to confess that I had all my life long been in ignorance and error.[6]

Calvin went on to say:

> I at length perceived, as if light had broken in upon me, in what a state of error I had wallowed, and how much pollution and impurity I had thereby contracted. Being exceedingly alarmed at the misery into which I had fallen, and much more at that which threatened me in the view of eternal death, I, as in duty bound, made it my first business to betake myself to thy way, condemning my past life, not without groans and tears.[7]

In his preface to his *Commentary on the Psalms* in 1557, he mentions his conversion as sudden:

> God by a sudden conversion subdued and brought my mind to a teachable frame, which was more hardened in such matters than might have been expected from one at my early period of life. Having thus received some taste and knowledge of true godliness, I was immediately inflamed with so intense a desire to make progress therein that, although I did not altogether leave off other studies, I yet pursued them with less ardour.[8]

---

6. Calvin, *Reformation Debate*, 88.
7. Calvin, *Reformation Debate*, 90.
8. Calvin, *Commentary on the Book of Psalms*, xl–xli.

French Calvinism in the Sixteenth Century

In October 1534, Calvin's return to Paris came at a significant and perilous escalation in the religious tensions of the time. This period marked the culmination of the Affair of the Placards, which occurred on October 18, 1534, across several cities, including Paris, Blois, Rouen, Tours, and Orleans. Radical Protestant factions disseminated placards that vehemently opposed the Mass, one of which bore the title "The Articles on the Horrible Abuse of the Papal Mass." Remarkably, one of these incendiary posters was affixed to the bedroom door of the king's residence at the castle in Amboise. In response to this provocative act, the king implemented a campaign of repression, resulting in the imprisonment of hundreds of Protestants. This atmosphere of persecution compelled key figures such as Calvin and Louis du Tillet to seek refuge first in Strasbourg and subsequently in Basel. Notably, other prominent reformers, including Cop, Guillaume Farel, Heinrich Bullinger, and Erasmus, were already present in Basel, the latter having passed away in 1531.[9]

Johannes Oecolampadius, who also died in 1531, had served in Basel as a professor of theology at the university, and his scholarly contributions became instrumental in the theological studies of John Calvin. Initially trained as a humanist, he had the distinction of being an assistant to the renowned Erasmus. Oecolampadius began his theological journey within the Lutheran tradition but subsequently adopted a more Zwinglian interpretation of the Eucharist, participating in the Marburg Colloquy of 1529. His treatise on ecclesiastical governance, although initially rejected by the city council, was later embraced by Martin Bucer in Strasbourg and subsequently influenced Calvin's work in Geneva. Notably, following his death, Oecolampadius's widow remarried the prominent reformer Wolfgang Capito, and after Capito's passing, she entered into marriage with Martin Bucer.[10]

It was at Basel that Calvin began to study theology in earnest. His desire was to find such a place where he could continue his studies unthreatened by such political disturbance. As a result, he revealed his identity to only a few friends, one of whom would later publish the *Institutes*: Thomas Platter. Here he virtually took a two-year independent study course in theology, which saw the first edition of the *Institutes* as its fruit.[11] Calvin wrote that he had a two-fold aim in composing the work: "first to vindicate from

---

9. Selderhuis, *John Calvin*, 34–58.
10. Fisher, *Christoscopic Reading of Scripture*, 14–27.
11. Gordon, *Calvin*, 47–62.

undeserved insult my brethren whose death was precious in the sight of the Lord and secondly, since the same sufferings threatened many pitiable men, that some sorrow and care for them should move foreign peoples." The first edition of the *Institutes* in 1536 was published by the press of Thomas Platter, and its introduction was addressed to François I and indicates that Calvin used this rhetorical device to make a case for the relaxation of French persecution of the Protestants. He explained:

> For this reason, most invincible king, I not unjustly ask you to undertake a full inquiry into this case, which until now has been handled with no order of law and with violent heat rather than judicial gravity. And do not think that I am here preparing my own personal defense, thereby to return safely to my native land. For though I regard my country with as much natural affection as becomes me, as things now stand, I do not much regret being excluded. Rather, I embrace the common cause of all believers, that of Christ Himself.[12]

Calvin went on to address the various charges leveled against the Protestant cause, which included claims of novelty, uncertainty, and the assertion that the true church had been long extinct.[13] The publication of his work generated considerable sales and popularity, especially compared to his work on Seneca. The initial printing sold out within a year, despite being written in Latin. This demand prompted a call for a revised edition, which Calvin did not complete until his exile in Strasbourg in 1538, and he added a French version in 1541. Calvin's return to France coincided with a temporary amnesty granted for Protestants. He remained there for six months but could not return on a permanent basis. Intent on resuming his scholarly pursuits in Strasbourg, accompanied by his brother Antoine and half-sister Marie, he encountered an unexpected turn of events. A conflict arising from the war between Charles V and François I necessitated a diversion southward to Geneva.

At this juncture, Geneva was engaged in strife with the Duchy of Savoy and had sought support from the Protestant city of Bern. Influenced in part by the evangelistic efforts of Guillaume Farel, on May 21, 1536, the male heads of households convened at the cathedral of St. Pierre and voted in favor of adopting an evangelical form of worship. Farel was informed of Calvin's impending passage through the city by his old associate Louis de

---

12. Calvin, *Institutes*, 2.
13. Calvin, *Institutes*, 3–11.

Tillet. Farel and his supporters desired to set up a more thorough system of discipline, worship, and education in Geneva, a task that Farel acknowledged exceeded his own capabilities.[14] Farel went to see Calvin and threatened him with God's judgment if he did not stay and help. Farel had a very strong personality and was twenty years older, so he practically bullied him into it. Calvin later said that Farel so frightened him that he felt that it was God himself speaking to him.

> Farel detained me at Geneva not so much by counsel and exhortation as by a dreadful imprecation which I felt to be as if God had from heaven laid his mighty hand upon me to arrest me ... He proceeded to utter the imprecation that God would curse my retirement and the tranquility of my studies which I sought, if I should withdraw and refuse to give assistance, when the necessity was so urgent. By this imprecation I was so stricken with terror, that I desisted from the journey I had undertaken; but sensible of my natural bashfulness and timidity I would bring myself under any obligation to discharge any particular office.[15]

Calvin thereby began by lecturing on the Epistle to the Romans. Shortly thereafter, he was appointed as one of the city's pastors. In January 1537, Calvin, in collaboration with Farel, drafted articles that outlined the church's governance, with a strong focus on discipline. These were submitted to the city council, which approved them but allowed only quarterly Eucharistic services rather than the recommended weekly observances. To educate children, Calvin promoted his Genevan catechism. Concurrently, Calvin also authored the *Instruction and Confession of Faith*, which summarized the foundational principles of the *Institutes*, designed for a lay audience. This effort culminated in a series of twenty-one articles aimed at countering the radical elements within the city with whom Calvin engaged in public debate, leading to their expulsion from Geneva in March 1537.[16]

However, opposition to the reform soon emerged from Pierre Caroli, a notable Parisian scholar who argued in favor of the efficacy of prayers for the dead while serving as a pastor in the neighboring city of Lausanne. His critiques of Calvin included efforts to undermine Calvin's colleague, Pierre Viret, in Lausanne. Caroli also accused Calvin and Farel of denying the doctrine of the Trinity. This conflict was then brought before the authorities

---

14. Manetsch, *Calvin's Company of Pastors*, 16–19.
15. Calvin, *Commentary on the Book of Psalms*, xlii–xliii.
16. Benedict, *Christ's Churches Purely Reformed*, 93–95.

in Bern, which supported Calvin and ordered Caroli's exile. Nevertheless, this incident significantly diminished Calvin's reputation within the community.[17]

Calvin's reforming endeavors also encountered a substantial setback during the elections of 1538, as four syndics opposed to Calvin were elected, favoring the reforms instituted in Bern. A pivotal issue arose concerning the use of unleavened bread in communion and the retention of baptismal fonts. While Calvin did not overtly oppose these modifications, he recommended postponing such changes until the controversy subsided. During the Easter service of 1538, Calvin and Farel refused to administer the Lord's Supper, and their sermons directly disobeyed the mandate to cease preaching until the issues were resolved. The heightened tensions culminated in a confrontation where swords were drawn, and Calvin and Farel narrowly escaped. The subsequent assembly of the Council of Two Hundred ordered their expulsion from Geneva.[18]

In the interim, Martin Bucer, a leading figure in the Reformation based in Strasbourg, extended an invitation to Calvin to serve as the French church's pastor, primarily dedicated to the numerous refugees fleeing persecution. Calvin's time in Strasbourg proved to be notably productive; he translated and revised Bucer's liturgy and collaborated with the esteemed French poet Clément Marot to produce a psalter, thereby introducing psalm-singing into the French church. Additionally, he revised and expanded upon the *Institutes*, leading to a new edition published in 1539. He authored a commentary on the Epistle to the Romans. He produced a treatise on the Lord's Supper, reflecting the influences of Bucer and adopting a conciliatory stance toward the Lutherans. Furthermore, Calvin traveled to Frankfurt in 1539 to engage with the Lutheran reformer Philipp Melanchthon.[19]

Calvin also married while in Strasbourg. In 1540, under the advice of Bucer, who saw him working so hard and wanted him to be better cared for. His marriage to Idelette of Buren, the widow of an Anabaptist, was an unromantic match. They had no surviving children of their own, but she did have two children that she brought into the marriage. She died in 1549. Calvin wrote to Farel of his desires in a wife: "I am none of those insane lovers who embrace also the vices of those they are in love with, where they are

---

17. Jenkins, *Calvin's Tormentors*, 17–30.
18. Manetsch, *Calvin's Company of Pastors*, 102.
19. Mullett, *John Calvin*, 79–102. On Calvin's sense of pastoral calling during his ministry in Strasbourg, see Quackenbos, "Calling in Conflict," 333–48.

smitten at first sight with a fine figure. This only is the beauty which allures me, if she is chaste, if not too nice and fastidious, if economical, if patient, if there is hope that she will be interested in my health."[20]

One of the most significant achievements in this period was Calvin's *Reply to Jacobo de Sadoleto*, the bishop of Carpentras who oversaw Roman Catholic efforts to woo the Genevans back to Rome. The bishop was a humanist scholar who emphasized the need for Christian unity as opposed to the squabbling that was taking place among the Protestants. The Small Council referred the letter to the Bernese, who sent it to Calvin asking him to reply. Calvin's response emphasized the sincerity of his conversion, salvation by faith alone, and the idea that the true church was comprised of true believers in Christ.[21] He explained, "All we have attempted has been to renew that ancient form of the church, which, at first sullied and distorted by illiterate men of indifferent character was afterwards flagitiously mangled and almost destroyed by the Roman pontiff and his faction."[22]

Calvin's reply was so well crafted that the Genevan Council asked him to resume his ministry in Geneva. The fact that supporters of Farel had gained control of the council in the 1540 election also contributed to the offer. However, Calvin had little interest in accepting the call. He was nicely settled in Strasbourg and had purchased citizenship in the city, which was required of all the clergy so they would be subject to civil law.[23] Returning to Geneva was not an easy decision for Calvin. He hated controversy and the previous struggle was extremely distasteful for him. He had an absolute dread for the city, saying in a letter to Pierre Viret on May 19, 1540, that he would rather die for eternity than suffer such torment in Geneva again.[24] Farel then again threatened him with God's judgment. After a long period of struggle, he consented to return, but he did not expect to spend the rest of his life there.[25]

When he returned to Geneva on September 13, 1541, John Calvin set up a committee charged with composing the Ecclesiastical Ordinances, which included an emphasis on stringent discipline. Within a month of his arrival, the Ordinances were enacted, outlining the roles of pastor, teacher,

20. Calvin, *Letters of John Calvin*, 107.
21. Calvin, *Reformation Debate*, 1–27.
22. Calvin, *Reformation Debate*, 62.
23. Mullett, *John Calvin*, 89–90.
24. Calvin, *Ioannis Calvini Opera*, 11: 36.
25. Gordon, *Calvin*, 121–23.

deacon, and elder. Additionally, they set up the Company of Pastors, facilitating weekly gatherings for scriptural study and theological discourse. At the same time, the Consistory—composed of elders and pastors—was designated to oversee ecclesiastical discipline. A point of contention regarding the Ecclesiastical Ordinances was the Consistory's authority in matters of excommunication. Although the scope of responsibility for excommunication was ambiguous, in 1543 the Council of Sixty articulated that while the Consistory could identify individuals for discipline, the actual enforcement of penalties would be the responsibility of the council. Such penalties often included exclusion from the quarterly celebration of the Lord's Supper.[26]

Calvin was known for his prolific preaching schedule, delivering sermons five times weekly—twice on Sundays, focused on the New Testament, and three times midweek, centered on the Old Testament.[27] He served as the presiding officer of the Company of Pastors, which met every Friday morning. The Consistory served as a liaison to the council, recommending penalties for immorality and theological error. Efforts towards moral reform led to restrictions on dancing and excessive drinking, including an initiative to replace taverns with clubs for patrons. Innkeepers took on an active role in monitoring community behavior; they were encouraged to report offenses such as blasphemy or insults, dancing, gambling, or singing lewd songs. Common crimes reported to the Consistory included absence from sermons, familial discord, critiques of ministers, card playing, the use of coarse language, and inappropriate behavior during sermons.[28]

The Consistory typically displayed leniency towards first-time offenders, often issuing mere admonishments. In some cases, the Consistory sanctioned divorce for biblically justified reasons, such as adultery or abandonment. However, repeat offenders faced significantly harsher punishments, including the imposition of the death penalty for adultery after a second offense, as well as for charges of heresy and blasphemy. In severe cases, torture was deemed permissible. Approximately three individuals were executed annually throughout this period, while about four faced banishments. Most cases addressed by the Consistory were relatively minor, with efforts made to reconcile interpersonal conflicts through physical

---

26. Manetsch, *Calvin's Company of Pastors*, 27–31, 193.

27. On Calvin's preaching, see Parker, *Calvin's Preaching*.

28. Watt, "Consistories and Discipline," 103–10. The consistory records during Calvin's tenure have been transcribed and published. See Watt and Watt, *Registres du Consistoire de Genève*.

gestures of reconciliation, such as handshaking. Individuals seeking admission to the Eucharistic service were required to recite the Apostles' Creed and respond to fundamental theological inquiries; failure to do so necessitated attendance at sermons and catechetical instruction.[29]

The stringent application of discipline motivated opposition to Calvin's leadership. One key adversary, Pierre Ameaux, a card manufacturer and member of the Small Council, objected to the prohibitions against card playing. Ameaux accused Calvin of being a false prophet and an Anti-Trinitarian, a charge reminiscent of the accusations levied against Calvin by Caroli in 1536. In a demonstration of authority, Calvin compelled Ameaux to publicly seek forgiveness by wearing a penitential garment, further igniting opposition.[30]

Another major opponent, Ami Perrin, initially a supporter of Calvin, turned against him following the Consistory's discipline of some of his family members. His father-in-law, François Favre, a prominent citizen of Geneva, faced excommunication for immorality, while Perrin's wife was exiled in 1553 for partaking in an illicit dance. Perrin also enjoyed wearing elaborate velvet clothing, which violated local regulations. Furthermore, he participated in secret discussions with King Henri II concerning a potential alliance between France and Geneva without the consent of the Genevan Council. As a syndic in 1553, he led a movement to limit the Consistory's authority. However, following the defeat of Perrin and his allies in the 1555 elections, they attempted an armed revolt, which ultimately failed, leading to their exile and a death sentence in absentia.[31]

In 1551, the former French Carmelite and physician Jérôme Bolsec participated in a weekly assembly known as the Congregation, which was characterized by Bible teaching and dynamic discourse among its members. During this gathering, Bolsec publicly challenged John Calvin's theology of predestination, labeling it unbiblical and suggesting it rendered God the architect of sin. In response, Calvin strongly denounced Bolsec, characterizing him as a tool of Satan, leading to Bolsec's imprisonment and subsequent trial. Ultimately, he was exiled and later authored a critical biography of Calvin, which served as fodder for Calvin's adversaries for many years. Notably, Bolsec accused Calvin of having been arrested for sodomy early in his career and claimed he suffered from severe lice infestation and

---

29. Manetsch, *Calvin's Company of Pastors*, 193–205.
30. Gordon, *Calvin*, 131–32.
31. Gordon, *Calvin*, 211–15.

genital crabs, stating that his body emitted a foul odor at the time of his death. Conversely, Théodore de Bèze's biography of Calvin disparagingly referred to Bolsec's wife as a prostitute. In time, Bolsec returned to the Roman Catholic Church, and his biography served as a piece of propaganda against Calvinism.[32]

Perhaps the most renowned case of ecclesiastical discipline in this era involved the Spanish scholar Michael Servetus, who was well versed in Hebrew, Latin, and Greek. His anti-Trinitarian perspectives appear to have been influenced by his interactions with Muslims and Jews who had been compelled to convert to Roman Catholicism. In July 1531, while in Basel, Servetus published *De trinitatis erroribus* (*On the Errors of the Trinity*), in which he argued that the term "Trinity" is absent from the biblical canon, viewing it as a later theological development rooted in Greek philosophical thought. He aspired to restore the unadulterated teachings of the early church, postulating that the Spirit of God descended upon the human Jesus during his conception. Consequently, he denied the eternal nature of the Son, referring to him instead as the "Son of the eternal God," while also rejecting infant baptism and the doctrine of original sin.

Servetus harbored a prolonged and contentious relationship with Calvin that can be traced back to 1534, when a potential meeting in Paris following the Affair of the Placards was rendered moot by Servetus's nonappearance. Adopting the pseudonym Michel de Villeneuve, which reflected his place of origin, he pursued a medical career and served as a physician to Archbishop Palmier in Vienne, France. Servetus subsequently stirred new controversy in 1553 with the publication of another religious text espousing further anti-Trinitarian views, entitled *Christianismi Restitutio*. This work can be seen as a direct refutation of Calvin's *Christianae religionis institutio*. Calvin commented to Guillaume Farel, dated February 13, 1546:

> Servetus lately wrote to me, and coupled with his letter a long volume of his delirious fancies, with the Thrasonic boast, that I should see something astonishing and unheard of. He takes it upon him to come hither, if it be agreeable to me. But I am unwilling to pledge my word for his safety, for if he shall come, I shall never permit him to depart alive, provided my authority be of any avail.[33]

---

32. Jenkins, *Calvin's Tormentors*, 152–73. For a lengthy blow-by-blow account of the Bolsec affair, see Holtrop, *Bolsec Controversy on Predestination*.

33. Calvin, *Letters of John Calvin*, 19.

French Calvinism in the Sixteenth Century

On April 4, 1553, Servetus was arrested and imprisoned in Vienne by Roman Catholic authorities, who labeled him a heretic. After a brief escape, he faced trial on June 17, where he was convicted of heresy by the Inquisition and subsequently burned in effigy. Although he initially intended to take refuge in Ferrara, his fascination with Calvin led him to Geneva, where he audaciously attended one of Calvin's sermons in disguise. Unfortunately for Servetus, he was recognized, apprehended, and charged with heresy. The accusations included denial of the Trinity and rejection of infant baptism. Calvin served as an expert witness for the prosecution, asserting that Servetus deserved death, albeit by beheading rather than burning. Ultimately, the city council exercised its authority, sentencing Servetus to execution by burning at the stake, after consultations with Protestant authorities in Zurich, Bern, Basel, and Schaffhausen.[34] As he was dying in the flames, his last words were allegedly "Jesus, Son of the Eternal God, have mercy on me."[35] To the very end, Servetus denied that Jesus was the eternal Son of God.

One should recognize that Servetus was at risk of persecution throughout the empire, as heretical beliefs were met with capital punishment universally. Had the authorities in Geneva chosen to banish Servetus rather than execute him, he would have likely met a similar fate elsewhere. Moreover, Geneva would have infringed upon imperial law by not executing a convicted heretic, potentially resulting in a reduction of its status, had the verdict diverged from that delivered in Vienne.[36]

Although John Calvin was not the only figure advocating for the execution of Servetus, some within the Francophone Protestant community believed that his actions had exceeded acceptable limits. Among the most prominent of these was Sebastian Castellio, an early advocate for religious toleration during a period marked by widespread intolerance. Castellio's education at the University of Lyon equipped him with proficiency in Latin, Greek, and Hebrew, as well as his native Italian and later German. After departing Lyon in 1540 for Strasbourg, he adopted the Reformed faith and subsequently made a significant impression on Calvin with his academic prowess.[37] Upon Calvin's return to Geneva in 1541, he offered Castellio a position as both teacher and rector at the Collège de Rive in Geneva. Castellio published his *Sacred Dialogues*, a series of discussions between

---

34. Jenkins, *Calvin's Tormentors*, 47–61; Bainton, *Hunted Heretic*, 142–48.
35. Jenkins, *Calvin's Tormentors*, 60; Calvin, *Ioannis Calvini Opera*, 14:657.
36. Gordon, *Calvin*, 222–23.
37. Jenkins, *Calvin's Tormentors*, 64.

biblical figures. This work gained considerable popularity across Europe, resulting in approximately twenty editions just during his lifetime.[38]

Despite these early successes, Castellio's salary was woefully inadequate to support his family.[39] Castellio sought a pastoral appointment, in part to improve his financial situation. His request was approved by the city council in 1543, but the Company of Pastors, following Calvin's lead, vetoed the appointment. The heart of Calvin's opposition stemmed from Castellio's rejection of the allegorical interpretation of Song of Solomon and a denial of Christ's descent into hell. Initially adopting a condescending demeanor towards Castellio, Calvin's stance shifted to a more hostile one as Castellio criticized Calvin's authoritarianism, ultimately labeling him a "beast."

Due to his defiance against Calvin's dominance, Castellio left Geneva for Basel, where he faced significant hardship, enduring years of poverty while working as a proofreader, translator, and manual laborer before eventually becoming a lecturer of Greek at the University. Castellio advocated religious freedom and the principle of conscience. He rejected the notion that individuals should be executed for differing biblical interpretations. Castellio's influence on the topic of religious toleration endured. The prevailing societal attitude towards the punishment of heretics was so entrenched that even many thoughtful Protestants failed to recognize the inherent immorality of thought repression. Few religious leaders within the Protestant tradition opposed the death penalty for heretics, with dissent often limited to objections regarding the misuse of such penalties rather than the principle itself.

In 1554, Castellio published, under the pseudonym Martin Bellius, *Whether Heretics Ought to be Punished*, a work that compiled arguments for toleration drawn from the writings of approximately twenty-five Christian authors, encompassing ancient and contemporary figures including Luther and Calvin. Castellio posited that the execution of heretics can have pitfalls, such as when a person is executed for heresy who is later discovered not to be a heretic at all. The other problem is to mete out a harsher penalty than Scripture demands. This contemplation underscores the complexity and ambiguity inherent in identifying heresy, illustrating the broader conflict between doctrine and individual conscience within the Reformation era.[40]

---

38. Bruening, *Refusing to Kiss the Slipper*, 141–42; Castellio, *Dialogi sacri*.
39. Naphy, *Calvin and the Consolidation of the Genevan Reformation*, 88–89.
40. Bellius, *De haereticis*, 12–16.

French Calvinism in the Sixteenth Century

The conflicts encountered by John Calvin during his career extended beyond his disputes with the Libertines, Servetus, and Castello. Notably, he attempted to reconcile doctrinal differences between Lutherans and Zwinglians concerning the nature of the Lord's Supper. Calvin sought to bridge the theological divide between Martin Luther and Ulrich Zwingli, affirming Zwingli's position that Christ is seated at the right hand of the Father. However, he argued that believers are spiritually elevated to commune with the risen Christ. Calvin rejected the idea, as Luther held, that Christ's physical body descends from heaven to be present on multiple altars simultaneously. Instead, he contended that through the power of the Holy Spirit, during the act of communion, believers are spiritually transported to heaven, partaking in a foretaste of the heavenly banquet.

In 1549, Calvin and Farel met with Heinrich Bullinger in Zurich. They hammered out the Consensus Tigurinus or the Zurich Consensus, which facilitated a coexistence of both Bullinger and Calvin's perspectives on the Eucharist. It was published in Zurich and Geneva in 1551. Notably, Bern only reluctantly endorsed the Consensus in 1551, leading to heightened tensions, given its role as the protector of Geneva. The inability of Luther's adherents to accept the Zurich Consensus resulted in a burgeoning schism: it faced severe criticism from Joachim Westphal, a Gnesio-Lutheran pastor in Hamburg, prompting an intense exchange of polemical literature between him and Calvin, characterized by acrimonious disagreement. Westphal argued that Calvin had changed his view from his 1541 *Short Treatise on the Lord's Supper* and his support for the 1540 *Variata* edition of the Augsburg Confession compiled by Melanchthon.[41]

The problem was that with an alliance with Zurich, Calvin lost support from the Gnesio-Lutheran party, which was inevitable since he never really agreed with the Lutheran position but was likely writing in a way to make his view more compatible. Luther and Calvin admired one another, even though Calvin was a generation younger. The two never met, but after reading Calvin's *Treatise on the Lord's Supper* in 1541, Luther said that Calvin was "a learned and godly man, and I might well have entrusted this controversy to him from the beginning. If my opponents had done the same, we should soon have been reconciled." Calvin wrote Luther a letter just before Luther died, but Melanchthon never delivered it to him, as he worried that Luther had become very cantankerous in his older years.[42]

---

41. On the debates between Calvin and Westfall, see Chung-Kim, *Inventing Authority*.
42. Brown, "Calvin and Luther," 299–309.

In 1559, John Calvin capitalized on the dissolution of the Lausanne Academy by playing a pivotal role in establishing the Genevan Academy, with Théodore de Bèze, who relocated from Lausanne in 1558, assuming leadership. Calvin presided over the inaugural service held at St. Pierre on June 5, 1559, during which Bèze delivered the opening address. The academy attracted several faculty members from Lausanne, contributing to its academic success. Calvin formulated the rules and regulations that governed the academy and was active in recruiting its faculty. The primary objective of this institution was to train ministers of the gospel, many of whom would go on to serve as pastors and play a significant role in the Reformed movement in France. Thus, Calvin's legacy endured well beyond his death in 1564, as this seminal institution continued to influence the international theological landscape.[43]

In 1563, John Calvin experienced a significant decline in health, which rendered him unable to preside over or participate in the fall Eucharistic service. Despite his deteriorating condition, he received visitors at his residence. He required assistance when he attended church to deliver sermons and was carried in a chair. Remarkably, Calvin continued composing his commentary on the book of Joshua, aided by his secretaries. He could partake in the Easter communion service in 1564—however, he passed away shortly thereafter on May 27, 1564.[44]

---

43. Maag, *Seminary or University*, 9–16. See also Kingdon, *Geneva and the Coming of the Wars of Religion*; Kingdon, *Geneva and the Consolidation of the French Protestant Movement*.

44. Gordon, *Calvin*, 332–33.

Chapter 7

Pierre Viret (1511–71)
Pastor and Professor

MARTIN I. KLAUBER

PIERRE VIRET SERVED AS one of the most significant figures of the Reformation, yet his legacy is relatively unknown in contrast to his more famous contemporaries such as John Calvin. Notably, Viret was not of French origin; he was born and raised in the Swiss territory called the Pays de Vaud in the small town of Orbe, about twelve miles north of Lausanne. It should be noted that the people in the western part of Switzerland spoke French, and as a result, they had strong ties to their French-speaking neighbors. His father was a tailor and a citizen but was not wealthy, yet the schools in the village were quite good. Young Pierre displayed exceptional academic abilities and was interested in ancient literature and theology. Marc Romain, who had studied with the Protestant reformers Wolfgang Capito and Martin Bucer in Strasbourg, was one of his teachers and began introducing Reformation ideas in town.[1]

This background provided a solid foundation for studying to become a Roman Catholic priest. In 1528, he likely attended the Collège de Montaigu, which was part of the University of Paris, where he learned to read the Bible in the original languages of Greek and Hebrew. He reportedly attended some of the lectures of the famed John Major, who taught at

---

1. Barnaud, *Pierre Viret*, 13–15.

Montaigu. Reformation ideas were being discussed and taught there, and Viret realized that he needed to reject the teachings of Roman Catholicism, which he compared to the superstitions of Babylon.[2] In 1530, however, he felt forced to leave Paris before completing his studies, perhaps because of opposition from the head of the Collège de Montaigu, Noël Béda, who became one of the major opponents of the Reformation.[3]

Returning to his hometown of Orbe, he met a man who would significantly influence his life, Guillaume Farel. Farel had been preaching the gospel throughout French-speaking Switzerland and had a gift for challenging young Christians to consider full-time ministry. With only a handful of followers of the reform in the town, Farel was preaching to a fledgling congregation of about ten people. When he noticed the young Viret in attendance, he encouraged him to consider becoming a pastor and an evangelist. Despite being only about twenty years old, Viret eagerly accepted this challenge. Farel ordained him to the ministry in 1531, and Viret began preaching immediately. Farel departed, leaving Viret in charge. Initially, only seven people joined the fledgling church and received communion on Easter Sunday. However, within a year, the congregation had grown to over seventy in a town with about one thousand inhabitants. Although he encountered much opposition from the Roman Catholics, the town council voted to accept the Reformation. To Viret's delight, his parents and likely his two brothers even decided to convert. Viret was not content to remain in one place and went to neighboring villages, where many favored the gospel. He was so effective that while he was on the road from Neuchâtel to Payerne, a priest who opposed his preaching attacked him, stabbed him several times, and left him for dead in a field. A passerby rescued him, but it took considerable time for him to recover.[4]

He later rejoined Farel and Antoine Fromment to preach in the city of Geneva, which had recently freed itself from the control of the neighboring Roman Catholic territory of Savoy. This liberation was achieved with the military help of the Swiss city of Bern, which had voted in favor of the Reformation in 1528. The Genevans depended on Bern's military protection and were subject to their benefactor's wishes on the nature of church reform. However, Geneva had not yet decided to move in favor of the gospel. Their preaching was so effective that they convinced the city council to

---

2. Bruening, "Pierre Viret," 18–20.
3. Barnaud, *Pierre Viret*, 16–35.
4. Linder, *Political Ideas of Pierre Viret*, 22.

vote in favor of the Reformation after a successful public disputation with a Roman Catholic representative. However, that did not mean that they did not have enemies in town. One of their adversaries poisoned Viret's spinach soup. Although he survived the poisoning, he suffered from stomach illness for the rest of his life.[5]

Viret then moved, after a brief period pastoring in Neuchâtel, to the neighboring city of Lausanne. His preaching there played a significant role in the city's acceptance of the gospel supported by Bern, which had annexed the territory. The Bernese held a public debate in October 1536 between the Catholics and the Protestants, with Viret and Farel representing the Protestants. John Calvin also briefly participated in the discussion. This debate, known as the Lausanne Disputation, lasted eight days. Historian Francis Higman has called this debate "the crossroads of the French Reformation," partly because it allowed the Protestants to articulate their beliefs clearly. They were so effective that even some Roman Catholic clergy were convinced and committed to the Reformed faith. One of the most critical issues at the disputation was the church's authority versus the authority of the Bible. Viret argued convincingly that the Bible was the higher authority and that the church must submit to it.[6]

Within a couple of weeks, the Bernese authorities decided to support the Protestants and declared that only Protestant worship would be permitted in the city. As a result, all the statues and paintings of the Virgin Mary, Christ, or the saints of the church had to be removed. The Protestants wanted to destroy these images because they believed that people were worshiping them rather than God. However, the methods proposed for removing these icons were controversial, since some advocated for their violent destruction.[7]

The Protestants also removed the communion altars, reminiscent of where Old Testament priests offered sacrifices to God, and replaced them with simple tables. Protestants accused their theological opponents of re-sacrificing Christ during the Mass. Catholics also thought that the bread and the wine were transformed into Christ's body and blood, meaning Christ would be physically present and worshipers would need to bow before him in worship. The Protestants disagreed and argued that Christ had

---

5. Linder, *Political Ideas of Pierre Viret*, 22–23.

6. Bruening, *Calvinism's First Battleground*, 141–42; Higman, "Dispute de Lausanne," 26–35.

7. Barnaud, *Pierre Viret*, 150–55.

already died and served as a once-and-for-all sacrifice for our sins. In their view, it would be an insult to his work on the cross to say that the Lord had to be re-sacrificed each time the Lord's Supper was practiced. They also discontinued the practice of the priests wearing special and elaborate clothing called vestments, which marked them off as an intermediary between God and man. They referred to their leaders as pastors, who wore simple black academic robes.[8]

Viret was called to serve as one of the pastors and a teacher in New Testament at the newly established Academy of Lausanne, a school for training pastors to minister in the French language. The head pastor and teacher in the Old Testament was Pierre Caroli, a controversial figure who had previously accused Calvin and Farel of denying the Trinity. Furthermore, Caroli advocated praying for the salvation of people who had already died, despite the biblical teaching found in Heb 9:27 that "people are destined to die once and after that to face judgment." Caroli was later dismissed from his positions, and Viret took his place.[9] This school was unique, as it was the only institution of its kind in French-speaking Europe, emphasizing the importance of training pastors to teach the Bible faithfully and accurately. Many churches in the territory surrounding Lausanne did not have a trained minister, making this school instrumental in serving those congregations.[10]

From January 1541 to July 1542, Viret served as a pastor in the neighboring city of Geneva. His friend John Calvin had been expelled from the city due to disputes with how the Bernese wanted to govern the church. The city council of Geneva followed Bern and instructed the pastors to use unleavened bread in communion. Calvin and Farel protested, arguing that this was a needless imposition by the civil magistrates over the church's governance, and they refused to serve communion on Easter Sunday in 1538. This caused great commotion in the church and the city, leading to Calvin and Farel's ouster. They initially took refuge in Basel, and then Calvin went to Strasbourg to pastor the French refugee church and Farel to Neuchâtel. Once Calvin was asked to return to Geneva in September 1541, Viret remained briefly to help him implement the reform.[11]

---

8. Bruening, *Calvinism's First Battleground*, 142.
9. Bruening, "Pierre Viret," 339.
10. Bruening, *Calvinism's First Battleground*, 174.
11. Linder, *Political Ideas of Pierre Viret*, 28–29.

Following Calvin's model, Viret returned to Lausanne and advocated for a stricter church discipline. Since the city had become Protestant by political decree, many people were still steeped in the religious superstition of the Catholic Church. Viret argued that the church, rather than the state, should determine who would be admitted to the communion service, a practice that would help root out such false beliefs. He wanted people to demonstrate that their beliefs and conduct were right before God. A passage in 1 Cor 11:27 says, "Whoever, therefore, eats the bread or drinks the cup of the Lord in an unworthy manner will be guilty of profaning the body and blood of the Lord." Viret wanted to prevent people from participating in an unworthy manner.

In contrast, the government authorities believed that allowing people to participate would bring them closer to God and that barring people should only be done in extreme circumstances. They emphasized the corporate fellowship among believers, while Viret emphasized each person's communion with the risen Christ. Viret kept pushing for a change in the procedure, and in 1558, he postponed the Christmas communion service. He wanted more time to examine the worthiness of individuals in participating. The leaders from Bern would not tolerate such action, and they expelled Viret and his followers from the town. Many faculty and students also left the school and relocated to Geneva to the newly founded Academy of Geneva. Viret relocated as well and served there for two years.[12]

Viret continued to struggle with poor health, and his doctors thought that the warm climate in southern France would be beneficial for him. He could secure permission to leave, but it was supposed to be temporary. He ministered first to the people in Nîmes for five months. Technically, he was still an employee of Geneva, as the Genevans paid his salary, and his family remained there. Viret's role was to observe the Protestant reform in southern France and report back to the Genevan authorities.[13] While in Nîmes, Viret faced the problem regarding images and icons in the church. Protestants considered these to be idolatrous because people tended to worship them instead of God alone. Viret wanted the images removed but opposed their violent destruction and suggested that any property stolen from the Catholics be returned to them. He still, however, agreed to preach in the cathedral. The highlight of his ministry came during the communion service held on Christmas Eve of 1561, where about eight thousand people

---

12. Bruening, "Pierre Viret," 344–45.
13. Roussel, "Pierre Viret en France," 810–11.

attended. He preached so effectively that several Roman Catholic authorities publicly professed the Reformed faith.[14]

After finishing his stint in Nîmes, Viret relocated to Montpelier for three months, where he consulted with medical doctors due to his poor health. During his stay, a civil war broke out in France between the Catholics and the Protestants. In June 1562, he accepted a request to come to Lyon, a major city the Protestants had just captured and controlled. He was planning a short trip there on the way back to Geneva, but the city leaders formally requested the Genevans to release him from his position, and they agreed. Viret officially became a pastor in Lyon, where in 1563, he served as the moderator for the National Synod of the French Reformed churches in France. In May 1563, the civil war was temporarily settled, and Catholics and Protestants were allowed to worship in Lyon. He had disagreements with some Catholic leaders. In August 1565, the King of France ordered that any pastors not born in France leave the country. Since Viret fell into that category, he was forced to leave Lyon.[15]

He remained in the country until early in 1567, when he accepted an invitation of Jeanne d'Albret, the Queen of Navarre, to introduce the Reformed faith to her kingdom in Béarn, a principality on the border with Spain in the Pyrenees mountains. He ministered there as a teacher and superintendent of the Academy of Orthez, overseeing the Reformed churches until he died in 1571.[16]

---

14. Linder, *Political Ideas of Pierre Viret*, 42.
15. Linder, *Political Ideas of Pierre Viret*, 45–50.
16. Chareyre, "Héritage de Pierre Viret en Béarn," 371–405.

Chapter 8

Peter Ramus (1515–72)
French Humanist

MARTIN I. KLAUBER

PETER RAMUS, ORIGINALLY NAMED Pierre de la Ramée, is noted for his significant contributions to philosophy and educational reform during the Renaissance period. Born in the small town of Cuts, located approximately five kilometers from Noyon—John Calvin's birthplace—in the Picardy region of northern France, Ramus's early life was marked by a complex socioeconomic background. He came from a family of noble origin; however, his grandfather, who lived in Liège in the Netherlands, was forced to flee following its destruction by Charles the Bold in 1468. As a result, he became a humble charcoal-burner in Cuts. Ramus's father, Jacques, managed to acquire a modest piece of land, transitioning into the role of a farmer. Despite the family's modest circumstances, Jacques ensured that his son was educated by a local schoolmaster, including his study of Latin. Tragically, Jacques's premature death left the family in difficult financial straits.[1]

Undeterred by these challenges, Ramus aspired to study at the University of Paris. Financial limitations, however, required him to return home on two separate occasions. His third attempt brought him to live with his uncle, a carpenter, in Paris, but he still did not have enough money to continue his studies. In a display of determination and humility, Ramus, at

---

1. Ong, *Ramus*, 18–20.

the tender age of approximately twelve, became a household servant to a wealthy student, the Sieur de la Brosse, at the Collège de Navarre—one of the university's constituent colleges. This position allowed him to pursue his studies during the evenings, an arduous but necessary schedule that exemplified his resilience and dedication to realizing his academic aspirations.[2]

During his studies at the Collège de Navarre, Ramus developed several significant friendships that would later prove instrumental to his academic and professional career. The most noteworthy was with Charles of Guise, who later became the Cardinal of Lorraine. The Guise family was extremely powerful within France, with a lineage that allegedly traced back to Charlemagne. Throughout the French Wars of Religion, the Guise family played a crucial role, leading the Roman Catholic faction in opposition to the Huguenots.[3]

Ramus demonstrated his affection for Cardinal Guise by dedicating many of his works to him. One must consider that Ramus was a Roman Catholic for most of his career, and the timing of his conversion to Protestantism is challenging to pinpoint. Some historians propose that his shift in religious allegiance occurred during the notable Colloquy of Poissy in 1561, while others contend that he did not formally engage in Protestant communion until 1569. His adherence to the Reformed faith probably occurred a mere two years before his tragic death during the Saint Bartholomew's Day Massacre.[4]

Due to the necessity of maintaining full-time employment while pursuing his studies during nocturnal hours, he exhibited a remarkable work ethic. One of his guiding principles was encapsulated in the Latin maxim *Labor improbus omnia vincit*, which translates to "hard work conquers all." He ultimately attained his Master of Arts degree at the age of twenty-one. While this age may not be considered unusually late by the standards of the time, it is noteworthy that, given the demands of his schedule, his academic achievements were particularly commendable.[5] His master's thesis caused a bit of controversy because of its title "Quaecumque ab Aristotele dicta essent, commentitia esse," which literally means that everything Aristotle has said is false. Some scholars have provided a more nuanced meaning that "whatever

---

2. Ong, *Ramus*, 20–21.
3. Carroll, *Martyrs and Murderers*, 131–32.
4. Waddington, *Ramus*, 130–38.
5. Skalnik, *Ramus and Reform*, 11–34.

Aristotle said is confused and contrived"[6] or "all the things that Aristotle has said are inconsistent because they are poorly systematized and can be called to mind only by the use of arbitrary mnemonic devices."[7] However, there is some doubt that Ramus ever publicly defended his thesis.[8]

He commenced his teaching career in philosophy at the Collège du Mans and subsequently at the Collège de l'Ave Maria, where he fostered a notable friendship with the esteemed scholar and rhetorician Omer Talon (1510–60). Talon was recognized for his academic prowess and as a staunch defender of Ramus against the critiques and rivalries he faced within the academic community. He began to challenge the prevailing teaching methods rooted in the philosophy of Aristotle. His stance was met with considerable resistance. Ramus's lectures culminated in the publication of significant works, including *Dialecticae partitiones*, *Dialecticae institutiones*, and *Aristotelicae animadversiones*. These texts exhibit a profound critique of Aristotle, characterizing him as not only a dubious sophist but also as a charlatan within the philosophical discourse.[9]

The critique of Cicero and Quintilian is clear in the discourse surrounding their rhetorical methodologies. The author points to what he believed are the shortcomings attributed to these figures, largely stemming from their integration of Aristotle's logical frameworks. Regarding Cicero, it was noted, "For he had transferred to rhetoric almost all Aristotle's obscurity concerning invention and arrangement, and indeed also style, confusedly making one art from the two, and then applying it confused in this way to the legal process of civil suits." Despite this criticism, he conceded Cicero's skill in eloquence, asserting that his rhetorical excellence stands without peer. Concerning Quintilian, Ramus asserted, "Quintilian follows Aristotle's and Cicero's confusion of dialectic and rhetoric. Indeed, he makes it worse by fabrications of his own, and by including in his teachings all the disputes concerning all the arts he had read or heard about—grammar, mathematics, philosophy, drama, wrestling, rhetoric." In contrast to these traditional interpretations, Ramus suggested a simplification of Aristotelian logic, advocating for its broader use beyond the confines of those scholars who wrote in Latin to those who preferred the vernacular.[10]

6. Skalnik, *Ramus and Reform*, 33–34.
7. Ong, *Ramus*, 46–47.
8. Ong, *Ramus*, 36–37.
9. Waddington, *Ramus*, 36.
10. Murphy, *Arguments in Rhetoric*, 10–81.

As a result, he was forced to debates his ideas publicly against a fellow professor. In the *Dialectique*, dedicated to the Cardinal Charles of Lorraine, Ramus defined dialectic as the art of disputing well in contrast to Cicero and Quintilian, who used the term as judging between alternatives.[11] He then divided dialectics into two parts, invention and judgment. Invention involves a systematic process of generating ideas and exploring information, while judgment relates to critical analysis, logical reasoning, and organizing ideas.[12] Although he defended himself ably, some of his opponents, including Jacques Charpentier, a professor of medicine, brought him up on civil charges of upsetting the entire curriculum of studies in 1544. The case went all the way to François I. The king issued an edict prohibiting him from teaching philosophy, and his books were banned from being sold in France. In the order, the king accused Ramus of being impudent and arrogant.[13]

In a display of resilience, Ramus dedicated himself to teaching mathematics and classical literature. In 1544, he became the chaplain at the Collège de Presles, where he also functioned as the institution's principal, as stipulated by the school's charter. This position granted him the authority to award scholarships, often to students bearing the same surname as Ramus, suggesting more than a bit of favoritism. He was also entrusted with the financial administration of the school, a responsibility he managed very well. His economic and academic skills not only facilitated the effective governance of the institution but also allowed him to secure a significant income. His colleague and friend Omer Talon joined him at the Collège de Presles and contributed to the academic discourse of the time by publishing an anti-scholastic treatise about rhetoric.[14]

When King François I died in 1547, the Cardinal of Lorraine, a longtime associate of Ramus, played a pivotal role in reversing the earlier edict restricting Ramus's academic pursuits. By 1551, the cardinal successfully persuaded the newly ascended monarch, Henri II, to grant Ramus the esteemed title of royal professor of philosophy and eloquence. In part this promotion helped to popularize Ramus's works, which sold quite well and underwent multiple printings. Ramus's innovative reinterpretation of Aristotelian logic sought to distill its complexities, rendering it more

---

11. Ramus, *Arguments in Rhetoric*, 1.
12. Ramus, *Arguments in Rhetoric*, 4.
13. Waddington, *Ramus*, 44–47.
14. Waddington, *Ramus*, 60.

comprehensible and accessible to a broader audience. Furthermore, he attempted to reformulate the entire liberal arts curriculum by outlining specific foundational purposes for academic disciplines. For instance, he asserted that the primary objective of geometry is to facilitate. He preferred self-evident axioms over syllogistic reasoning, opting to transition from broader concepts to specific instances. He also employed charts to elucidate his ideas further. While syllogisms are practical in addressing uncertain concepts, the strategic use of axioms can facilitate more effective discourse. The implementation of Ramist charts proved to be instrumental in enhancing reader comprehension and promoting the dissemination of his methodological framework.[15]

After his appointment as a royal professor, Ramus delivered an inaugural address to a crowd of more than two thousand. The lecture hall was so crowded that several individuals reported having difficulty breathing. Ramus thrilled the audience with his dynamic speech. However, not everyone was entranced by his skills, and some regarded him as an egomaniac and a buffoon. In 1557, King Henri II appointed Ramus to serve on a commission dedicated to the reform of the curriculum at the University of Paris. The findings of this commission were subsequently published in 1562 under the title *Avertissements sur la réformation de l'Université de Paris*, which included a Latin version of the treatise. In this work, Ramus fervently criticized what he believed were the exorbitant costs associated with higher education. A principal concern he raised was the abundance of staff and professors, many of whom continued to teach after attaining their master's degrees. Ramus proposed a significant restructuring of the financing of education; he argued that rather than students bearing the burden of faculty salaries, the crown should instead assume responsibility. Since the king was already financing the regius professors, he reasoned that it would be logical to extend this financial model to encompass the broader faculty, thereby alleviating the financial strain on students and potentially boosting the accessibility of higher education. His goal in reforming the curriculum was to simplify it and make it more accessible to the public. He disparaged the distinction between theory and practice and emphasized that the arts and sciences needed to be useful in life.[16]

In 1561, Ramus attended the Colloquy of Poissy, during which Théodore de Bèze and his Protestant colleagues engaged in a dialogue with

---

15. McKim, "Function of Ramism," 506.
16. Skalnik, *Ramus and Reform*, 51.

Roman Catholic apologists regarding various theological issues, particularly emphasizing the nature of Christ's presence in the Eucharist. Ramus was seemingly impressed by the Protestant delegation's presentations, leading to speculation that he may have converted. Despite this potential transformation, he remained hesitant to declare any Protestant affiliation. He continued attending mass and maintained a devout lifestyle and lifelong celibacy. His subsequent flight from Paris to Fontainebleau, under the protection of the king from 1562 to 1563, further points to the likelihood that Ramus was at least suspected of harboring Protestant sympathies. It was not until 1569 that Ramus openly identified as a Protestant, participating in a Reformed celebration of the Eucharist in Heidelberg—an act that signified a critical shift in his theological alignment, given that involvement in such a service was by no means a foregone conclusion.[17]

During the French Wars of Religion in 1568, Ramus vacated his position in Paris and sought academic opportunities abroad. He undertook lectures and engagements at various Protestant educational institutions in Strasbourg, Bern, Zurich, Heidelberg, and Geneva. When he visited Geneva, he encountered significant opposition from Théodore de Bèze, who perceived Ramus as a disruptive influence, particularly due to his critiques of Aristotelian logic. Bèze, a proponent of Aristotelian categories in theological discourse, refused to offer Ramus an academic position, reflecting the limited acceptance of Ramus's controversial methodologies within the broader Protestant academic community at that time. The absence of offers from Protestant academies abroad further underscores the nascent status of his approach to logic and education on the international stage.[18]

Upon his return to Paris in 1570, the relationship between Ramus and the Cardinal of Guise had already deteriorated significantly, leading to a loss of the latter's support. This decline is understandable in the context of the intense sectarian conflict represented by the ultra-Catholic faction during the French Wars of Religion. Following this setback, Ramus experienced a temporary reinstatement to his former position. In his appeal to the cardinal, he asserted that the latter had previously encouraged him to engage with the writings of the church fathers, which subsequently led Ramus to adopt a conviction aligned with the Reformed tradition. However, this rationale proved ineffective in persuading the cardinal to restore his patronage.[19]

---

17. Graves, *Peter Ramus*, 73–78.
18. Skalnik, *Ramus and Reform*, 111.
19. McKim, "Ramus in History and Theology," 233.

His conversion to Reformed Christianity proved costly for Ramus, not just in his profession career but for his very life. During the Saint Bartholomew's Day Massacre, a gang of thugs broke into his apartment on August 26, 1572. They shot and stabbed him to death and threw his body out of the window, where it was decapitated and thrown into the Seine.[20]

While one wonders what additional works Ramus may have published had he lived longer, he did have one theological work printed after his death, the *Commentariorum de Religione Christiana* (1576). His former student Théophile de Banos prepared the manuscript and honored his teacher by publishing it and including a brief biography of Ramus. In this important work, Ramus described theology as an *ars* or *doctrina bene vivendi*, framing it as the art or doctrine of living well rather than merely the study of the divine. This perspective emphasizes that the inquiry into doctrine is pursued with a practical objective, transcending the pursuit of knowledge for its own sake. Ramus's approach proved particularly beneficial for theological study, as he divided the field into two principal components: doctrine and discipline. The Puritans made great use of his method and combined theological principles with practical application. Furthermore, Ramus's framework was useful for writing sermons, enabling preachers to transition from evident axioms derived from Scripture to more specific moral and ethical applications relevant to the lives of their congregants.[21]

He published more than fifty titles, predominantly in Latin, although a select few were composed in French. Notably, his most famous work, *Dialecticae Institutiones*, achieved considerable popularity, with nearly 250 editions produced. Despite facing resistance to his methodological approach in certain places, such as Geneva, his contributions resonated significantly with subsequent generations of theologians. Among these, English Puritans manifested a particular affinity for his methodology, with William Perkins emerging as a prominent advocate of his ideas. The influence of Ramism can also be seen in the development of Reformed theology in colonial New England. He also had followers throughout Europe in the Netherlands, Germany, France and Switzerland.[22]

---

20. McKim, "Ramus in History and Theology," 233.

21. McKim, "Function of Ramism," 508–9.

22. See Tipson, "Seeing the World though Ramist Eyes," 275–92; Miller, *New England Mind*; Sharratt, "Ramus 2000," 399–455; McKim, "Function of Ramism," 503–17; McKim, *Ramism in William Perkins' Theology*.

Chapter 9

Gaspard de Coligny (1519–72)
Huguenot Admiral

MARTIN I. KLAUBER

GASPARD II DE COLIGNY, later named Lord of Châtillion, was a member of the French nobility and the leader of the Huguenot military during the French Wars of Religion. He was the third-born son of one of the most influential and powerful families in the country. His father was Gaspard I de Coligny, Marshall of France, and his mother was Marie Louise de Montmorency. Her brother, the Constable Anne de Montmorency, was an extremely prominent man who owned an incredible amount of land in France.[1] Anne was a common man's name in those days, and he served as young Gaspard's patron and supporter. As Constable, he was the supreme commander of the French military. Young Gaspard's older brother, Pierre, died young, and his second older brother, Odet de Châtillon, became a cardinal in the Roman Catholic Church at the young age of sixteen. It was not uncommon for young men of high noble rank to be named to such a position. Gaspard I died in 1522, when his son was only three years old, and the constable took the young Gaspard II as a kind of ward.

When Marie Louise was named lady in waiting for Queen Claude, the wife of King François I, the family moved to the royal court, where Gaspard II received a classical humanist education to help prepare him for

---

1. On the Constable Anne de Montmorency, see Rentet, *Anne de Montmorency*.

a military career. The real power in France rested in the great noble houses. The monarchy was controlled by the Valois line, with Henri II being the king, but he died in a jousting accident in 1559. Henri's wife was Catherine de Medici, from Florence, and three of her sons became kings, with her serving as the queen mother. The other houses included the Bourbons, who were closely related to the Valois; the Montmorencys; and the Guises. The House of Guise was based in Lorraine and was extremely powerful in wealth and political influence. Its key figures were François de Lorraine, the Duke of Guise, and his brother Charles, Cardinal of Lorraine. Their sister was Mary of Guise, who married James V, the King of Scotland, and was the mother of Mary Queen of Scots.[2] The Châtillions were much less wealthy and influential, but Coligny allied himself to the constable, who was the head of the Montmorency clan.

As a young man, Coligny served as an officer in the French military. He served the kings François I and Henri II and did such an excellent job as a military officer during the French wars in Italy that he was rewarded with various titles and honors. In 1551 he was named Governor of the Île de France, the area surrounding and including Paris. He also received the post of admiral, which was not related to any naval service but was a title of prestige second only to the office of constable which was held by his uncle. Then, in 1555, he received the governorship of the province of Picardy, an area just north of Paris.[3]

Coligny was led to the Protestant faith in part by his younger brother, François d'Andelot, who became a Huguenot while a prisoner of war and sent a book of Christian devotion to Gaspard. Gaspard read the book eagerly and was impressed by the truth of the Reformed faith and the honesty of Andelot's belief. However, his conversion did not come easily. John Calvin wrote a letter to him in September 1558 that indicates that Gaspard had not yet given his life to Christ. But Calvin encouraged him to diligently read the Bible and to dedicate himself to God's service. By 1559, it was reported that he had stopped attending Roman Catholic services. It was not until 1561, when he had his son baptized according to the ritual of the Reformed churches, that it was clear that Gaspard had committed himself to the Protestant Reformation. It was illegal for Protestants to hold their church services except in the private estates of the nobility. Gaspard, however, fought against the restriction, and on Palm Sunday, the Sunday before

2. Salmon, *Society in Crisis*, 122.
3. Carroll, *Martyrs and Murderers*, 76.

Easter, he held a Protestant service in his home. He had finally convinced the king to allow private services.

Gaspard also hired a Reformed pastor to officiate at church services held at his estate. It was common for members of the aristocracy to hold worship services not only for themselves but for their households and others who wanted to come. They would sing the psalms loudly in the French language, which were composed by some of the best poets of France. In those days, it was also risky to commit to the Reformed faith, as France was almost completely Roman Catholic.[4] Protestants believed that attending the Mass was an act of superstition because the Roman Catholics thought that the bread and the wine of the Lord's Supper were magically changed into the literal body and blood of Christ, so they worshiped the bread and wine, even though it still looked and tasted like bread and wine.

The death of King Henri II in a jousting accident on June 30, 1559, during the celebration of the Treaty of Cateau-Cambrésis, was a tragedy that changed the destiny of France. Henri II was succeeded by three of his young sons, who needed supervision. The first was François II, who was dominated in the royal council by the Duke of Guise and the Cardinal of Guise, both virulent opponents of Protestantism, which they considered heresy. The Guise clan had plenty of rivals for control of the council, most prominently Henri II's widow and the Queen Mother, Catherine de Medici.[5] On the opposite end of the spectrum were the Protestant leaders Antoine de Bourbon, King of Navarre, and Louis de Bourbon, the Prince de Condé.

Some Protestants decided to either liberate the king from the Guises, as the Catholic faction would describe it, or to free him, as the Protestants argued, from their control. This attempt occurred at the king's castle in Amboise, located on the Loire River, on March 17, 1560. Jean du Barry, Seigneur de la Renaudie, along with several hundred armed men, tried to storm the castle. However, they were defeated by forces led by the Duke of Guise, who had been warned about the operation. Du Barry was captured, drawn, and quartered, and between 1,200 and 1,500 of his followers were executed, with the bodies hanging from hooks on the castle walls or trees for the townspeople to view. This so-called Conspiracy of Amboise had the support of Louis de Bourbon, who was arrested. Coligny was more moderate, however, and opposed the plot.[6]

---

4. Shimizu, *Conflict of Loyalties*, 24–30.
5. Holt, *French Wars of Religion*, 42.
6. Salmon, *Society in Crisis*, 126.

Everything changed on March 1, 1562, when the Duke of Guise, who strongly opposed the Protestants, came across a group of Huguenots worshiping in a barn in the town of Vassy, in northwestern France. Guise and his supporters quickly attacked the five hundred or so worshipers who were singing the psalms. About fifty of the Protestants were killed and their pastor was wounded and arrested. Then, when the Duke of Guise went to Paris, the people gave him a hero's welcome, even though he had murdered so many innocent people. A mere two months later, the Duke of Guise was assassinated, and many, especially from the House of Guise, believed that Coligny was behind the murder, in part because the assassin implicated him under torture. François's son Henri then succeeded him as the Duke of Guise and held Coligny personally responsible.[7]

At this point, war between the Catholics and Protestants in France began with Coligny commanding the Protestant armies. It may seem strange that these two groups, who both claimed to be Christians, would resort to armed conflict, but each thought that the other had turned against God. The Bourbon family joined with the Protestants, led by Henri de Navarre. He was the king's cousin and in the line of succession for the French throne. The Catholics were led by the Guise family, with the Montmorencys staying within the Catholic fold but trying to straddle the fence between the two sides.

In 1570, at the Battle of Jarnac, the Prince de Condé was murdered by Catholic troops after surrendering. Coligny was left as the chief commander of the Protestant sources. This was followed by the Peace of Saint-Germain-en-Laye which provided Coligny the opportunity to regain favor at the royal court. In September 1571, Coligny was readmitted into the king's council at the royal estate in Blois and was provided a sizable pension. He pursued a policy of war with Spain that held the possibility of Catholics and Protestants joining against a common enemy.[8] However, most of the council were against the plan and feared that Coligny would use his military to attack the Spanish Netherlands.[9]

Amid all this conflict, Coligny got remarried in 1571 to Jacqueline de Montbel d'Entremont, a widow with land holdings in Savoyard territory who had converted to the Reformed faith. His first wife, whom he married

---

7. Salmon, *Society in Crisis*, 147.
8. Knecht, *French Religious Wars*, 26.
9. Salmon, *Society in Crisis*, 185–86.

in 1547, was Charlotte de Laval, a noble woman from a prominent house in Brittany. She died in 1568, having borne him at least eight children.[10]

The two sides continued fighting each other until 1572, when a compromise was reached. The Queen Mother, Catherine de Medici, agreed to an arranged marriage between her daughter Margaret de Valois and Henri de Navarre. He was the king's cousin and in the line of succession for the French throne. Navarre had to convert to Roman Catholicism for the marriage to take place, and the upcoming nuptials were unpopular with both Catholics and Protestants.[11]

Coligny was invited to the wedding, which took place in Paris. It was a grand affair, and many of the French nobility, Catholic and Protestant, were invited. However, this was a time of great religious discord in Paris, and Coligny was right in the middle of it. Passions had been inflamed over the relocation of a stone pyramid topped with a crucifix from the home of the Huguenot merchants Philippe Gastines and his son Richard to a Roman Catholic cemetery. They had been executed, the house torn down, and their property confiscated. Their crime had been using the house to host illegal Protestant worship services, and the funds taken from the estate were used to make the site into a public park. There was a law that required the destruction of all monuments that had slandered the Protestants. The Gastines family asked Coligny to take the case before the royal council to have the cross removed and the property returned to the family. The compromise stipulated that it be moved to a cemetery, which was done late at night in December 1571. The cross had been a symbol of Roman Catholic power and its removal angered many in the city. The Protestants countered by saying that the symbol had not been destroyed but moved to a much holier place in a cemetery. The Protestants probably underestimated the impact that the relocation of the cross would have on the Roman Catholic population in Paris and that anger would be directed toward Coligny, since he brought the case to the crown.[12]

After the wedding was over, Coligny stayed in Paris for a few days on important business for the security of France. While Coligny was walking to his apartment, Charles de Louviers, Sieur de Maurevert, who had been a page for the Guise family in his youth and had briefly converted to Protestantism in 1569, shot him from a window of a building on the street and

10. Whitehead, *Gaspard de Coligny*, 34–35, 233.
11. Knecht, *French Religious Wars*, 29.
12. Kingdon, *Myths*, 39–40.

injured his hand and elbow. If he had allegedly not just bent down to tie his shoe, he probably would have been killed. Maurevert, who received pensions from the new Duke of Guise in 1573 and later from Henri III in 1575, escaped while Coligny was recovering from his wounds in his home.[13] The king sent his personal doctor to tend to him, and the king even visited him and promised to bring the shooter to justice. However, on August 24, in the morning, soldiers under the command of the Duke of Guise broke into his home, killed him, and threw him out the window. The Duke of Guise allegedly turned the body over to make a positive identification. Coligny's head was severed, and the mob mutilated and dragged his body through the city feet-first, threw it into the Seine, and then pulled it out again. Then they hung it upside down from the Gibbet of Montfaucon, which was the main gallows used by the king of France at that time. They left the body hanging for several days so the birds could pick at it until members of the Montmorency family removed it secretly by night.[14]

The big question for historians is, Who ordered Gaspard to be murdered? He had many enemies, especially from the leaders of the Guise family who despised the Huguenots and blamed him for the murder of François, the Duke of Guise. Most historians blame the Queen Mother, who had turned against Gaspard in part for his desire for the French to fight a war against Spanish forces in the Netherlands. She was against the war, possibly because she feared that it would increase the power of the Protestants since Coligny would lead the war effort. In either case it would have taken an order from the king, Charles IX. However, he was quite young at twenty-two and was strongly influenced by his mother. It is quite possible that the Queen Mother pressured the king to give the order, but the evidence is hardly conclusive.

Coligny's assassination marked the beginning of a series of coordinated assaults on Huguenot leaders. However, these attacks quickly spiraled out of control, leading city authorities and mobs of local citizens to engage in widespread killing and looting, targeting not only known Protestants but also individuals with whom they had personal grievances. The attackers identified themselves with white crosses, a symbol that had been embraced by Catholics since 1567. Despite the focus on Protestants, some Catholics also fell victim to the violence. Among the deceased were many prominent Protestant figures, including renowned author Peter Ramus, Comte de la

---

13. Carroll, *Martyrs and Murderers*, 208–10.
14. Holt, *French Wars of Religion*, 82–84; Whitehead, *Gaspard de Coligny*, 269.

Rochefoucauld, and Charles de Téligny, who was Coligny's son-in-law. Early victims after the assassination of the targeted nobles included members of the Gastines. Richard Gastines's widow was murdered in front of her two young children, and the relatives of Jacques Gastines were also killed.[15]

The killing then became indiscriminate, with any suspected Huguenots being targets. Men, women, and children of all social classes were indiscriminately stabbed, shot, or clubbed to death, their bodies stripped, mutilated, and dragged to the Seine, where they were dumped into the river.[16] It is difficult to determine how many people were murdered but, after a week of chaos in Paris, about two thousand Protestants had died.[17]

Coligny had been the primary target of the killings, but his death was symbolic of the massacres that took place in Paris. The Wars of Religion continued without him, but his memory remained firm among the Huguenots. In 1889, a monument to Coligny was erected in Paris across the street from the Louvre, a testimony of his remarkable life and tragic death.

15. Holt, *French Wars of Religion*, 86.
16. Treasure, *Huguenots*, 172.
17. Diefendorf, "Prologue to a Massacre," 1067; Buchanan, "Massacre of St. Bartholomew's," 66.

Chapter 10

Théodore de Bèze (1519–1605)
Reformer and Scholar

STEPHEN M. DAVIS

THÉODORE DE BÈZE (BEZA) was an important and remarkable figure in the French Reformation, a supporter of Calvin and his successor as the moderator of the Company of Pastors in Geneva. As a pastor, theologian, poet, writer, and diplomat, he worked tirelessly to advance and strengthen the Reformation in a turbulent period of European history. He was influential in the conversion of Jeanne d'Albret, Queen of Navarre, and was a confidant of her son Henri IV. Bèze remained loyal to the king and considered the protection of Protestants by the Edict of Nantes in 1598 a grand achievement even with Henri's conversion to Catholicism. He requested, along with Farel, the Duke of Wurttemberg's intervention for the Waldensians and represented French churches at the conference in Worms in 1553, where he affirmed agreement with the Lutheran Confession of Augsburg, except for the Lord's Supper.[1]

Bèze was born in Vézelay into a noble family of Nivernais, a former province in central France, and from childhood was placed in the care of one of his uncles. At his baptism, his first name was Dieudonné and hellenized later during his studies in Paris.[2] Throughout his life, he remained

---

1. La Tour, *Origines de la Réforme*, 167.
2. Hamon, *Siècle et demi d'histoire protestante*, 63.

attached to his natal village and signed most of his books *Theodorus Beza Vezelii*.[3] He was born the year Charles V became Holy Roman Emperor and was a contemporary of Catherine de Medici, François de Guise, Guillaume Farel, Gaspard de Coligny, and of course John Calvin. At the age of nine, he was sent to the school of Melchior Wolmar, a German intellectual, and was under his tutelage until the age of sixteen. Wolmar was imbued with Reformation principles, and his knowledge of ancient languages enabled him to discern the truths the Reformers were promoting. He had communicated his views to Bèze, whose writings as a young man expressed his resolve to identify with the Reformed faith. However, Bèze did not make an open profession, perhaps because his master left France in 1535, and Bèze left for Orléans, initially to study law. He was then more attracted to literature, in which domain he completed his studies.

At the age of twenty, he went to Paris, where he gained a reputation for his poetry and appears to have forgotten the views of Wolmar. A collection of risqué poetry entitled *Juvenilia* contained scandalous verse that he was forced to remove, and he was pressured to enter into an ecclesiastical vocation. A serious illness afflicted him almost to the point of death and brought about serious reflection on his lifestyle. Bèze left for Geneva and once removed from family pressure and worldly concerns, he was brought back to the earlier teachings he had forgotten. Having renounced ecclesiastical advantages and other financial benefits bequeathed by his uncles, he married Claudine Denosse, with whom he had been secretly engaged for four years. He accepted an offer to teach Greek at the Academy of Lausanne, where Pierre Viret and Mathurin Cordier became his colleagues and remained in this post for about ten years.[4]

While still a professor in Lausanne, he was sent, along with Farel and Jean Budé, to request the intercession of German princes before the French Court in favor of four hundred Reformed believers who had been arrested and imprisoned by Henri II. Seven of them had already been burned at the stake. The intercession was successful, and the prisoners were released. During this time, Bèze encountered Melanchthon in Frankfurt. Although all their theological views were not in harmony, they established a lasting friendship. On his return in 1558, he went from Lausanne to Geneva. He was received there as a minister, and a strong friendship grew between him and Calvin. Their friendship was lifelong, and Bèze concluded his biography

---

3. Weben, *Théodore de Bèze*, 9.
4. Bèze, *Histoire ecclésiastique*, i–iv; Hamon, *Siècle et demi d'histoire protestante*, 66–67.

of Calvin's life with these words: "I can now declare, that in him all men may see a most beautiful example of Christian character, an example which it is as easy to slander as it is difficult to imitate."[5]

Calvin established the Academy of Geneva in 1559, where many ministers completed a cycle of studies. Bèze was appointed a professor at the Academy and then rector. Students studied biblical languages and followed the commentaries of Calvin and then later of Bèze. He "was a specialist in Greek, with a knowledge of biblical Greek that probably surpassed Calvin's. He was also a fine writer of Latin, one of the best Latin poets of his century."[6] Once students had acquired a solid basis of theological understanding, they were sent to rural parishes of Geneva and Lausanne as interns to serve as deacons, school teachers, or pastors.[7] Calvin held the conviction that the Psalms of David were the most appropriate for singing in churches. Among his many accomplishments, Bèze completed the work that Clément Marot began years earlier and in 1562 published the first editions of a complete Psalter with one hundred and fifty psalms.[8]

Bèze's former colleagues then requested his presence in France to intercede on the behalf of Protestants before French princes and obtain guarantees of protection. The House of Guise, sworn enemies of Protestants, exercised great control over the young King François II (r. 1559–60), successor to Henri II, and sought the assistance of Spain and Rome to counter the influence of the *princes du sang* of the House of Bourbon.[9] The Guises were at the center of intrigues and attempts to rid the kingdom of Protestants. The Duke of Guise engaged in subterfuge with German Lutherans and pretended to be favorable toward the Confession of Augsburg to separate Lutherans from French Protestants. His mother, Antoinette de Bourbon, shared her son's antipathy toward the Huguenots and was displeased to see the spread of Calvinism in the region.[10]

François II died on December 5, 1560, after a reign of only eighteen months. His brother Charles IX (r. 1560–74) became king at the age of ten, and their mother Catherine de Medici became queen regent.[11] Catherine

---

5. Bèze, *Life of John Calvin*, 115.
6. Kingdon, *Myths*, 152.
7. Garrisson, *Histoire de protestants*, 78.
8. Doumergue, *Vrai chant*, 45.
9. Bèze, *Histoire ecclésiastique*, vi–viii.
10. Stéphan, *Épopée huguenote*, 107.
11. Félice, *Histoire des protestants*, 111–12.

understood the growing influence and power of Protestantism and sought an accord with the Calvinists. Persecuting them was not without risks due to the number of provinces where they were in the majority, and noblemen and generals were counted among them. It was one of those moments when the Reformation might have become dominant, humanly speaking, had it not been for the maneuvers of Catherine, the ambition of the House of Guise, the intrigues of the king of Spain, and the opposition of the Catholic clergy. A word already in use for several years to designate Reformed militants became more widely adopted in the French language. Bèze and the Cardinal de Lorraine began using the term "Huguenot" in their correspondence, possibly referring to the Swiss word *Eidgenossen* (Confederation). It was applied to Reformed believers as confederates or collaborators under the orders of Geneva.[12]

Catherine called a conference in the royal city of Poissy on September 9, 1561, to which Protestant leaders were invited before the king, the royal court, and Catholic prelates. The Protestant delegation had ten pastors and twenty-two lay leaders, led by Bèze, who was sent in Calvin's place. After speeches from the king and chancellor, the delegates from the Reformed churches were introduced. Bèze eloquently expounded Calvinist doctrine and presented the king with a copy of the Reformed Confession of Faith. At the second session on September 16, Catholics explained their views on the same points of doctrine. The Cardinal de Lorraine's speech was marked by brilliance and courtesy in a true spirit of reconciliation. There was much common ground on the doctrines of God, the Trinity, the incarnation, and the Person and work of Christ. Areas of discord involved the sacraments and the government of the church. The pope's legate, Hippolyte d'Este, arrived from Rome and reminded the cardinals of the church's authority and its opposition to Gallicanism. Despite the disagreements, Bèze, the Bishop of Valence, and the Cardinal de Lorraine submitted an agreed-upon text to Catherine on October 1. She saw in this the possibility of avoiding civil war between the two confessions. However, the theologians of the Sorbonne condemned the text, declaring it heretical.[13]

Bèze's description of the Reformed understanding of the Eucharist as the spiritual presence of Jesus Christ was considered scandalous. One cardinal called upon Catherine to either silence the orator or allow all the Catholics to leave the chamber. The Catholic delegation demanded that

---

12. Babelon, *Henri IV*, 83.
13. Hamon, *Siècle et demi d'histoire protestante*, 67–70.

the Reformed representatives unconditionally accept the authority of the Catholic Church and its teaching of the Eucharist that the elements, bread and wine, are transformed into the body and blood of Christ (transubstantiation). If they refused, they were threatened with anathema and banishment. At this same conference, the Jesuit representative, Jacques Lainez, in a discourse that astonished even many Catholics, compared the heretics to foxes and wolves who did not deserve a hearing. The conference ended on October 9, and any hope to unite the two religious confessions through mutual concessions turned out to be an illusion.[14]

Bèze assisted Chancellor Michel de L'Hôpital in writing the Edict of January in 1562 under Catherine de Medici, which emboldened Protestants to worship publicly.[15] The Catholic Church opposed the edict and went on the offensive, leading to the massacre of Protestants in Vassy in the Champagne region in 1562 the following year, which signaled the beginning of the Wars of Religion. On Sunday, March 1, the Duke of Guise learned that several hundred Huguenots were meeting in a barn at a time when Reformed worship was forbidden in cities. With two hundred armed men, he came across this large congregation gathered at a short distance from the Catholic Church and attacked them. Accounts of the number of victims vary; some estimated at least fifty or sixty killed and two hundred wounded. After a supposed investigation into the massacre, the story was invented, casting the Huguenots as the aggressors. The duke was received in Paris with a triumphal entry, and Catholics compared him to Judas Maccabee as the defender of the faith.

The Protestant consistory of Paris sought justice and sent Bèze to the royal court. Antoine de Bourbon, the King of Navarre and a convert from Protestantism to Catholicism, accused the Huguenots of attacking the duke. In an audience with Catherine and Charles IX, Bèze declared, "Sire, it is true that the Church of God, in whose name I speak, receives beatings but does not give them; but may you also be pleased to remember that this church is an anvil that wears out many hammers."[16] The massacre at Vassy was followed by another massacre at Sens in Bourgogne the following month. Protestants had opened a place of worship on March 29 outside the city. This was unacceptable to Catholics. The attack took place

---

14. Félice, *Histoire des protestants*, 133–36.

15. Babelon, *Henri IV*, 94.

16. Hamon, *Siècle et demi d'histoire protestante*, 72; Félice, *Histoire des protestants*, 150–53.

on April 12 after a Catholic procession as the Protestants left their church service. Massacres and pillaging went on for several days, resulting in over one hundred victims. Bodies attached to wooden planks were thrown into the river. Thus began the Wars of Religion.[17]

When the first war of religion broke out, Bèze attached himself to Louis de Condé. After his multiple amorous escapades, the prince had earned himself the reputation of a man of war and was recognized by Queen Elizabeth I of England (r. 1558–1603) and German princes as the leader of the Reformed movement, based on his name and qualities.[18] Bèze was present as a minister at the Battle of Dreux and his enemies wasted no time in falsely accusing him of taking up arms and having blood on his hands. He ably defended himself against these calumnies and no proof was offered for the charges against him. After this battle, Bèze followed Admiral de Coligny and returned to Geneva only after the Peace of Amboise ended the war in 1563.[19] Later in life, he lamented that though armed defense was just and necessary, he prayed that God would give his people the grace in the future to suffer martyrdom rather than take up arms.[20]

One year after his return to Geneva, Bèze experienced one of the most difficult times of his life, with the death of Calvin in 1564. Bèze seemed like the only one able to take the place left by Calvin and would remain in Geneva almost without interruption until he died in 1605. He was named moderator of the Company of Pastors and was reelected annually until 1580. According to Elton, Bèze "inherited [Calvin's] near-papal position, and Geneva was to preserve Calvin's constitution and principles for some 150 years."[21] Bèze consecrated himself to writing works on the government and administration of the church. One of his most significant publications was *Histoire ecclésiastique des églises réformées au royaume de France* (*Ecclesiastical History of Reformed Churches in the Kingdom of France*), which detailed events advancing or hindering the Reformation in France from 1521 to 1563. His works also included *Annotations of the New Testament* and his Greek text that influenced the Geneva Bible and the King James Bible respectively.[22] He "published no fewer than nine editions of the Greek

---

17. Hamon, *Siècle et demi d'histoire protestante*, 5–6.
18. Babelon, *Henri IV*, 150.
19. Bèze, *Histoire ecclésiastique*, xvii–xviii.
20. Hamon, *Siècle et demi d'histoire protestante*, 72.
21. Elton, *Reformation Europe*, 162.
22. Scrivner, *New Testament in Greek*, vii.

Testament between 1565 and 1604" and appears "to have been the first scholar to collate the Syriac New Testament."²³

He returned to France for family matters in 1568, participated in the Synod of La Rochelle in 1571, and was elected moderator of the assembly. Jeanne d'Albret; her son Henri de Navarre, future king of France; and Louis de Condé were present. After the Saint Bartholomew's Day Massacre in 1572, Rome publicly thanked God for the success of this dark plot while Bèze labored to find places of refuge for his co-religionaries who had escaped the slaughter. Refugees were received with open arms in many places where Bèze had written to German princes to welcome them. In 1574, *Droit des magistrats sur leurs sujects* (*On the Right of Magistrates over Their Subjects*) was published anonymously, although "contemporary insiders knew and a few outsiders suspected that its author was Theodore Beza. . . . Archival evidence uncovered in Geneva in more recent times has decisively confirmed this fact."²⁴ The term "magistrate" was used in the general sense of those holding authority. He insisted, along with other writers of his time, on the concept of a social contract between subjects and governing powers.²⁵

Bèze became "the acknowledged if informal leader of the French Protestant movement" and "used this position, as had his predecessor Calvin, to welcome to Geneva practically any refugee of the Reformed faith who could make it to the city's walls."²⁶ According to Kingdon, Bèze traveled to Germany in 1574 "to advise a new Prince de Condé, son of his former patron, on plans for a fourth war of religion against the French crown. *Du droit des magistrats*, therefore, can be regarded to some degree as propaganda designed to lay the groundwork for that new war."²⁷

Bèze traveled on several occasions, including the colloquies of Montbéliard in 1586 and Bern in 1588. The colloquy in Montbéliard was convoked by Count Frédéric de Montbéliard, who had welcomed a great number of refugees in his territory and desired that they unite with his subjects, who professed the Lutheran Confession of Augsburg. The colloquy ended without a union of confessions, but Bèze encouraged Reformed believers to participate in the Lord's Supper with Lutherans if their participation did not require them to renounce their religion. The colloquy in Bern

---

23. Metzger and Ehrman, *Text of the New Testament*, 151–52.
24. Kingdon, *Myths*, 151.
25. Babelon, *Henri IV*, 325.
26. Kingdon, *Myths*, 11.
27. Kingdon, *Myths*, 153–54.

took place shortly after the death of his wife Claudine Denosse, to whom he had been married for forty years. There he managed to resolve tension over the subject of predestination. Upon his return to Geneva at the age of seventy, he married a widow, Catherine de la Plane.[28]

In the spirit of the times, Bèze's life was marked by religious intolerance. He defended the execution of Michael Servetus in 1553 for the crime of heresy.[29] In his preface to the *Histoire de la vie et mort de Calvin* (*History of the Life and Death of Calvin*), he exclaimed that "there are few cities in Switzerland and Germany where Anabaptists have not been rightly put to death."[30] There was also opposition to Calvinism at the end of the sixteenth century. Jacob Arminius (1560–1609), after his studies at the University of Leiden, spent time in Geneva with Bèze before accepting a pastorate in Amsterdam. Neither Arminius nor Bèze lived to see the confrontation in Protestantism between Arminianism and Calvinism at the Synod of Dordt in 1618 and 1619 and the persecution that followed.[31] The small Republic of Geneva was claimed by the Duke of Savoy after the Treaty of Cateau-Cambrésis in 1559 and resisted repeated assaults from the armies of Charles Emmanuel. In 1602, at the age of eighty-three, Bèze rose up to encourage the inhabitants with his sermons on the sufferings and the resurrection of Christ. Every December, Genevans celebrate the night of the Escalade, when the city repulsed an attack by the Duke of Savoy's army in its attempt to scale the city's wall.[32]

Toward the end of his life, Bèze began to lose his short-term memory but conserved the memory of those things learned in his youth. He died in Geneva surrounded by his colleagues. In his last will and testament, he asked his colleagues for forgiveness for his faults, expressed wishes for their happiness, and exhorted them to live in peace. His ashes were disposed at the cloister of Saint-Pierre rather than the cemetery of Plein-Palais due to hatred against him and the fear that his enemies might dig up his body and send it to Rome. After his death, his adversaries published defamatory works against him. Cardinal Richelieu in his *Méthode* brought unsubstantiated accusations against him, erroneously claiming the accusations were found in Protestant writings. From his enemies, his attachment to the

---

28. Bèze, *Histoire ecclésiastique*, xviii–xxi.
29. Panetta, "Heresy and Authority," 63.
30. Cottret, *Histoire de la Réforme Protestante*, 10.
31. Cottret, *Histoire de la Réforme Protestante*, 296.
32. Weben, *Théodore de Bèze*, 15.

Reformation earned him charges of felonies and treason, and he was called the "shame" of France.[33]

Among his followers, Théodore de Bèze became known as the "Bronze Horn," joining Antoine de Chandieu (Silver) and Calvin (Gold) in the triumvirate of Reformed leaders.[34] Bèze was "widely respected for his contributions to the Reformed movement" and "was probably best known for his work in biblical studies and theology."[35] He authored over a hundred works on theology, poetry, history, controversies, and a voluminous correspondence. When he died on October 13, 1605, Protestants in France lived under the protection of the Edict of Nantes. His influence on Protestantism was immense, but France would remain a firmly Catholic kingdom, and the rights of Protestants would not last.

33. Bèze, *Histoire ecclésiastique*, xxii–xxiii.
34. Van Raalte, *Silver Horn*, 6–7.
35. Kingdon, *Myths*, 152.

Chapter 11

Pierre de la Place (c. 1520–72)[1]
Huguenot Martyr

MARTIN I. KLAUBER

PIERRE DE LA PLACE was a notable early Huguenot reformer who was killed just days after the Saint Bartholomew's Day Massacre in 1572. Hailing from Angoulême, his family held significant social standing. His father, also named Pierre de la Place, was a local mayor and served as a financial advisor to Louise de Savoie, the Regent of France and mother of King François I. He played a critical role in arranging the marriage between François I and Claude of France and in negotiating the king's freedom following his capture at the Battle of Pavia in 1525.

The young Pierre de la Place studied law at Poitiers, where he encountered a young John Calvin and completed his studies at Paris. By 1542, La Place gained recognition for paraphrasing parts of the *Institutes of Justinian*, a work circulated among his peers before publication in 1546. Starting his legal career at the Parlement of Paris at the young age of twenty-two, La Place quickly garnered respect, leading King François I to appoint him as his attorney at the Court of Aids. This tribunal addressed matters of public finance and customs duties and was located in the Palais Vieux in Paris. He eventually advanced to the position of President of the Court of Aids. While practicing law, he studied Calvin's writings and examined the

---

1. Adapted from the author's introduction to *Right Uses of Moral Philosophy*.

differences between Roman Catholicism and Reformed theology, initially refraining from committing to either side. He no doubt initially hesitated to embrace the Reformed faith openly due to the potential repercussions for his career and personal safety.[2]

Charles IX was an eleven-year-old king, and his mother, Catherine de Medici, the widow of Henri II and Queen Mother, was taking charge. However, she struggled to manage the competing noble factions divided along religious lines. She had four sons, three of whom would eventually become kings, and she faced the challenge of steering the monarchy through significant political strife. The biggest threat to her authority came from prominent noble factions who sought to control the royal council, notably the House of Guise. François, the Duke of Guise, and Charles, the Cardinal of Lorraine, held considerable power over the young king and dominated the royal council. Conversely, the Protestant faction was represented by leaders like Antoine de Navarre, King of Bourbon, and Louis de Bourbon, Prince de Condé. The Guise faction advocated for the harsh suppression of Protestantism in France, actively guiding royal policies toward that end. The Huguenots recognized these dangers, and the Prince de Condé was prepared to confront the Guises.[3]

Such action took the form of an attempt to liberate the king from the Guises by kidnapping him, as the Catholic faction would put it, or freeing him, as the Protestants contended, from their control. The attempt occurred at the king's castle at Amboise on the Loire River when Jean du Barry, Seigneur de la Renaudie, along with several hundred armed soldiers and members of the nobility, attempted to storm the castle on March 17, 1560. They were defeated by the forces led by the Duke of Guise, who had been tipped off in advance about the operation. Too many people were in on the secret plans, so they inevitably leaked out. Du Barry was captured, drawn, and quartered, and between 1,200 and 1,500 of his followers were executed, with the bodies hanging from hooks on the castle walls or trees for the townspeople to view. This so-called Conspiracy of Amboise had the support of the Prince de Condé, even though the Genevans, led by Calvin, attempted to discourage the plot. Condé was eventually arrested in October of 1560 for his role in the affair and was set to be put to death when the king died in December from an ear abscess. The new king was his younger brother Charles IX, and Catherine de Medici took advantage

2. Haag and Haag, *France protestante*, 6:312.
3. Holt, *French Wars of Religion*, 45–48.

of the situation by removing the Guises from power and releasing Condé from prison. The entire affair was a disaster for the Protestant cause, as it confirmed for many in France that they were, indeed, seditious.[4]

In 1561, the Queen Mother took a moderate stance, disappointing the Guise faction. She appointed Antoine, the King of Navarre, who had a legitimate claim to the regency as the first prince of the blood, as Lieutenant-General of the realm. This made him the second in military command, following Constable Anne de Montmorency. Additionally, she included Gaspard de Coligny, a Huguenot who had not supported the Conspiracy of Amboise, in the royal council. In response to these appointments, on Easter Sunday 1561, François de Guise; Anne de Montmorency; and Jacques d'Ablon, Marshal of St. André, formed a coalition known as the "Triumvirate," which aimed to protect the Roman Catholic faith with help from Philip II of Spain.[5]

On April 19, Catherine issued an edict at Fontainebleau that allowed limited tolerance for the Huguenots, permitting them to worship freely in their homes. However, the Protestants sought the right to build their churches and to hold public worship services. In retaliation, the royal council and the Parlement of Paris prohibited even private worship and offered a general amnesty for earlier violations of religious laws. Consequently, the Queen Mother's edict never went into effect.[6]

In response to ongoing religious tensions, Catherine, aided by Chancellor Michel de L'Hôpital, convened the Colloquy of Poissy in September 1561 to explore the possibility of a theological compromise. The Protestant side was represented by Théodore de Bèze and Peter Martyr Vermigli, alongside a group of twelve theologians. The Roman Catholic delegation was comprised of six cardinals and thirty-eight bishops and archbishops. Charles IX and the royal family attended to foster some agreement to ensure peace. However, the theological divides were too significant for any real resolution. Bèze gave the first comprehensive speech, attempting to highlight common ground, but when he discussed Christ's physical presence in communion, he controversially stated that it was "as far away from the bread and wine as the highest heavens are from the earth." This provoked cries of *"blasphemavit!"* from the prelates. Shortly after, papal legate Ippolito d'Este, the Archbishop of Ferrara, along with Diego Laynez,

---

4. Holt, *French Wars of Religion*, 43–45.
5. Knecht, *French Wars of Religion*, 30.
6. Knecht, *French Wars of Religion*, 30.

General Superior of the Jesuit order, arrived to undermine the Colloquy's objectives. Despite efforts to reconcile the two faiths based on the Confession of Augsburg, an agreement proved unlikely.[7]

In January 1562, the Queen Mother issued the Edict of Saint Germain, granting Protestants the right to hold peaceful worship services outside the city in rural areas. However, it prohibited them from bearing arms or worshiping at night to prevent potential uprisings, marking a significant advancement for the Huguenots. The Parlement of Paris resisted the registration of the edict, prompting the young king to forcefully order its approval, which was eventually done in March 1562.[8]

The momentum toward conflict intensified following the Massacre of Vassy on March 1, 1562. On that day, François, the Duke of Guise, accompanied by his entourage, was headed to Sunday Mass near his estate in northeastern France. They encountered a group of Huguenots worshiping in a barn. When Guise attempted to enter forcefully, the Huguenots pushed back, throwing rocks, one striking the duke. In retaliation, he ordered the barn to be set ablaze, resulting in the deaths of at least fifty worshipers and over a hundred injuries. The incident sparked a range of reactions from outrage to disbelief among Protestants, prompting many in the Huguenot nobility to prepare for military action out of fear of further attacks. They organized under leaders such as Admiral Gaspard de Coligny and Louis de Condé. Condé claimed that the young king and his mother were effectively prisoners of the Guises and took control of the city of Orléans on April 2, 1562.[9]

In the midst of this religious and political chaos, La Place carefully evaluated the implications of his beliefs. Remaining in the Roman Catholic faith would have been more beneficial for his career, yet he was a committed Protestant. He realized he would be better off leaving Paris for Picardy, where his family owned land. After losing his position at the Court of Aids, he used this opportunity to study Christianity more thoroughly alongside the works of classical authors. He also tended to his land and educated his children, expressing a strong desire to provide them with a solid Christian education and hoping to write brief treatises to aid in this effort. According

---

7. Knecht, *French Wars of Religion*, 30–32.
8. Holt, *French Wars of Religion*, 48–49.
9. Holt, *French Wars of Religion*, 49–50.

to Émile and Eugéne Haag, his work, *Droict usage de la philosophie morale avec la doctrine chrestienne*, was created for this purpose.[10]

Additionally, he published *Traitté de la vocation*, dedicated to Charles IX, which was translated into English in 1578. In his dedication, La Place advised Charles IX that a crucial trait of effective leadership is selecting wise advisors and officials. He argued that a discerning monarch must recognize which public servants are motivated by self-serving or dynastic interests at the expense of the realm. La Place opposed Cicero's view that a person's vocation stems from their spirit, natural inclinations, and chance. Instead, he maintained that divine providence, rather than fate, guides one toward their true calling. Notably, La Place asserted that God has a vocational calling for everyone, regardless of their profession. While he endorsed hereditary succession as a suitable means of choosing a monarch, he criticized the Roman Catholic approach to selecting clergy, recalling a time when the laity had a role in calling individuals to serve. For instance, in Num 8:10, the Levitical priests were presented to the Israelites for consecration before being offered to God.[11]

La Place's work featured an interesting section on the kingdom's management during periods of royal minority. He recognized that the Salic law barred women from reigning independently but noted it did not prevent them from taking part in the kingdom's administration. He specifically acknowledged the legitimacy of Catherine de Medici as queen mother, commending her governance as divinely inspired, and regarded her as wise, good, and virtuous.[12] While his favorable view of Catherine likely had little impact on his return to Paris or on fostering greater religious tolerance for Protestants, it likely contributed positively to his cause. La Place returned to Paris in 1563 following the Edict of Amboise, or Edict of Pacification, which Catherine de Medici signed on behalf of Charles IX. Hugues Daussy mentions that La Place anonymously wrote *L'Epistre au roy, sur la faict de la religion* (1564), in which he contended that the edict fell short in safeguarding the rights of Huguenots.[13]

La Place managed to rebut the accusations against him to the extent that Charles IX reinstated him to his previous position. Following this, the Prince de Condé appointed him to manage his household affairs, akin to a

10. La Place, *Du droict usage de la philosophie morale*, 6:312.
11. La Place, *Traitté de la vocation*, 1–12.
12. La Place, *Traitté de la vocation*, 36–37.
13. Daussy, *Parti Huguenot*, 538.

modern chief of staff.[14] During his time with Condé, La Place recognized the importance of creating a comprehensive account of the origins of the religious wars in France, eventually broadening it into a history of the conflicts under Henri II, François II, and Charles IX. Emile and Eugène Haag noted that this work was surprisingly balanced, rather than simply serving as Protestant propaganda, although it did favor Huguenot perspectives.[15]

Myriam Yardeni has observed that La Place was quite subtle in his wording. For instance, when discussing Bèze's address at the Colloquy of Poissy, he described him as "modest," which was likely inaccurate. He quoted Bèze's speech extensively, offering only summaries or fragmented citations of the Roman Catholic representatives, Cardinal François de Tournon and the Cardinal of Lorraine. He did not directly criticize the papacy but adopted a more constructive approach, documenting from a Gallican viewpoint and using a historical narrative to create a convincing, empathetic account. He stressed that religious belief is fundamentally a matter of personal conscience and little connected to the Huguenots' loyalty to the crown, even though religion and politics were deeply intertwined and personal belief was a fundamental right that would take years to actualize. The mistreatment and denial of the Third Estate, a concern also echoed by Michel de l'Hôpital, the royal chancellor, were highlighted in his work.[16]

La Place wrote his *Right Use of Moral Philosophy* as a brief introduction on the subject for his children. Still, it also aimed to demonstrate the superiority of a distinctly Christian—particularly Protestant—view on moral philosophy and its application in the public sphere. The first edition of this work, which serves as the basis for this translation, was published in 1562 in Paris and included a dedication to Michel de L'Hôpital, the Chancellor of France from 1560 to 1568. A second edition followed in Leiden in 1568. La Place enjoyed a positive relationship with L'Hôpital, who had previously been President of the *Chambre des comptes* from 1555 to 1560. L'Hôpital was a sympathetic figure, as he facilitated the registration of the Edict of Romorantin by the Parlement of Paris, which aimed to protect suspected heretics from secret inquisitorial trials. His motivation stemmed probably from a desire to foster a general reform within the French church

---

14. Haag and Haag, *France protestante*, 6:313.

15. Haag and Haag, *France protestante*, 6:313; La Place, *Commentaires de l'estat de la religion et république*.

16. Yardeni, *Minorités et mentalités*, 60–62.

that would lead to unity between Reformed and Roman Catholic factions. Thus, the persecution of Protestants was counterproductive to this goal.

Furthermore, L'Hôpital set up a meeting of the Council of Notables to encourage the convening of the Estates-General, which eventually took place after the death of François II. This assembly helped to lay the groundwork for the Colloquy of Poissy and the Edict of Saint-Germain in 1562, granting greater tolerance to the Huguenots. However, L'Hôpital faced opposition from papal legate Ippolito d'Este, primarily due to his challenges to the Council of Trent's authority and his Gallican views on royal power. He also had disputes with the Guise faction, particularly with the Cardinal of Lorraine, concerning the effects of implementing the Decree of Trent on the peace achieved with the Protestants. After the Massacre at Vassy, L'Hôpital briefly withdrew from court until the reconciliation efforts in Amboise in 1563. Some historians, like Albert Buisson, have speculated that he was a secret Protestant. Still, according to Seong-Hak Kim, such claims were likely based on an uncritical interpretation from contemporary Protestants who believed he aligned with their beliefs. Kim contends that L'Hôpital advocated for religious tolerance to maintain order in the realm. Both Bèze and Calvin suggested that if L'Hôpital were indeed a secret Protestant, he should be open about it and recognize his value for the Reformed cause.[17]

The dedication of La Place's treatise to L'Hôpital aimed to encourage him to adhere to Scripture as the basis of civil law, which is an aspect of divine law. Natural law serves as a foundation for civil law but is subordinate to divine law. One issue with natural law is its frequent corruption due to humanity's sins. To reform natural law, a return to Scripture, which outlines God's ultimate justice, is necessary. La Place began his introduction by addressing the potential conflict of entering theological discussions given his legal background, yet he emphasized the significant connection between divine law and justice. He argued that theology is crucial for achieving true justice and understanding the law. While acknowledging philosophy's role in knowledge acquisition, he referenced Tertullian to note that its combination with theology can lead to errors; thus, philosophy should defer to theology and the Scriptures.[18]

The *Commentaires* was initially published without an author's name, but Jean-François Gilmont has demonstrated that La Place was indeed the

---

17. Buisson, *Michel de L'Hôpital*, 12; On Michel de l'Hôpital see Kim, *Michel de l'Hôpital*; Kim, "'Dieu nous garde,'" 595–620.

18. La Place, *Du droict usage*, x.

author. While the publisher wasn't specified, Gilmont argues convincingly that Eloi Gibier, the official printer for the Prince de Condé, was responsible for its release. According to Daussy, this work began several historical defenses for the Reformed cause, highlighting the repression in 1557. It was crafted in a narrative format to appeal to a broader audience.[19] Patrick Cabanel pointed out that the book's chronological beginning was deliberately chosen to follow the narrative established by Johann Sleidan, who passed away in 1556 and authored the significant *Commentaries on the State of Religion and the Republic under Emperor Charles V* (1556).[20]

La Place's work underwent multiple editions, published in Rouen, La Rochelle, and Paris. Written from a Huguenot perspective, La Place's treatise lamented various acts of persecution, starting with the arrest of over a hundred Protestants who were gathered for worship in a private home on September 4, 1557, in Paris's Latin Quarter. Among those arrested were several noblewomen sent to Châtelet prison. He also provided a detailed, sympathetic account of Anne du Bourg, a Calvinist member of the Parlement of Paris who advocated for religious tolerance but was arrested for heresy and executed on December 23, 1559. La Place carefully conveyed Du Bourg's defense strategy, cleverly using Du Bourg's words instead of his own. Du Bourg asserted that he believed solely in the Bible's divine inspiration, arguing that Roman Catholic doctrines he opposed contradicted Scripture. He illustrated that God worked for six days, rested on the seventh, and sanctified the Sabbath, pointing out that the pope had introduced additional fast days contrary to this principle, restricting the occasions when the faithful could consume meat. He also criticized clerical celibacy, suggesting that it exceeded Paul's instructions in 1 Cor 7, which states that only those with a special gift of continence should refrain from marriage.[21]

La Place presented a Protestant interpretation of the history of religious conflicts. His work went through seven editions, was translated into Latin between 1575 and 1577, and into English in 1573. It was later included in the 1836 multi-volume anthology, *Choix de chroniques et mémoires sur l'histoire de France*.[22] Regrettably, the onset of the third phase of the Wars of Religion forced him to leave Paris again in 1568. His home was ransacked, his library dispersed, and his finances were frozen. This time, he

---

19. Daussy, *Parti Huguenot*, 45.
20. Cabanel, *Histoire des protestants en France*, 241.
21. La Place, *Commentaires*, 5–6, 26–29.
22. Buchon, *Choix de chroniques et mémoires*.

took refuge at a castle in Valois owned by his nephews, where he worked as a tutor to their children. While at the castle, a warrant was issued for his arrest due to his Protestant beliefs and rumors about him, prompting him to escape and hide in the forest. Eventually, he found shelter with a compassionate neighboring lord who allowed him to stay in his castle in isolation, with only the Bible to read.

During this time, he wrote his work *Traicté de l'excellence de l'homme chrestien et manière de le cognoistre*, which was published posthumously in 1575 and translated into English in 1576.[23] He dedicated this work to the Queen of Navarre, Jeanne d'Albret, a prominent Huguenot. In it, he powerfully presented traditional Reformed doctrines like election, emphasizing that it was God's special love and favor that chose and set apart individuals for salvation long before their existence. He argued that the excellence of a Christian man lies not in oneself, contrary to the philosophers' perspective, but solely in God's grace that unites a person with Christ and leads to regeneration. Once the persecution against Protestants calmed with the Peace of Saint-Germain on August 5, 1570—ironically brokered by Jeanne d'Albret—he returned to his home and his position at the Court of Aids. However, his time there proved unstable and concluded in 1572 with the Saint Bartholomew's Day Massacre.

A scholar's legacy is usually not marked by their death. Still, in the case of La Place, his end was notably recorded in Simon de Goulart's *Mémoires de l'État de France sous Charles IX* as well as in a lithograph of his murder by Joseph Martin Kronheim, featured in the 1887 edition of *Foxe's Book of Martyrs*. Consequently, he gained more recognition for martyrdom than his life's work. Goulart's three-volume publication significantly highlighted the experiences of Huguenot martyrs between 1570 and 1574. It served, in part, as a propaganda tool for Protestant resistance.

Living quietly on the outskirts of Le Marais, La Place first learned about the massacre from a French captain named Michel, who visited his home to inform him of the imminent danger he and other Huguenots faced. The captain offered shelter but inquired about the amount of gold in the house, seemingly as a request for payment. La Place responded that the king would not allow such behavior, prompting the captain to suggest taking him to the king. Recognizing this as a trap, La Place declined and escaped through a back exit. He did, however, pay an official one thousand crowns to ensure the safety of his wife and children with a Catholic

---

23. La Place, *Traicté de l'excellence*.

family. Unfortunately, Pierre could not find anyone nearby willing to hide him from the authorities and eventually returned home, where his wife had already returned. While worshiping at home on a Sunday with his wife, relatives, and servants, ironically discussing the book of Job and reading Calvin's commentary on it, they were interrupted by the arrival of Provost Senescay and archers, sent under the king's orders to deliver him to the Louvre for protection. However, on the way, the group was attacked, and the soldiers offered no resistance as La Place was stabbed to death. They took the body to the stable at the Hôtel-de-Ville, where it was thrown into the Seine. His home was subsequently looted, with suspicions arising that a rival named Stephen de Neuilly may have played a role in orchestrating the murder as he took over La Place's official roles.[24]

---

24. White, *Massacre of St. Bartholomew*, 423–25.

Chapter 12

Jeanne d'Albret (1528–72)
Huguenot Queen

STEPHEN M. DAVIS

JEANNE D'ALBRET, ALSO KNOWN as Jeanne III, established the Reformed religion in Béarn, an autonomous region at the time in southwestern France. She reinforced the region's independence from the French Crown after her mother Queen Marguerite de Navarre had laid the foundation there for Protestantism. Apart from her, there was little sincere practice of religion among the Bourbons, who have been described as "high-living aristocrats who enjoyed the pleasures of the flesh too much to be convincing representatives of Calvinism."[1] Unlike her mother, Jeanne "openly confessed her faith leaving no doubt about her religious affiliation."[2]

Jeanne was born in 1528 at the Château of Saint-Germain-en-Laye, the only daughter of Henri II d'Albret and Marguerite d'Angoulême and baptized in the château's chapel. Of her three other siblings, two sisters died at birth, and a brother Jean died two months after birth. Ill health followed Jeanne throughout her life. In her early years, she was confined to the Château of Plessis-lès-Tours and suffered from the absence of her parents. Her father Henri and her uncle King François I showed her great tenderness, and she became known as *la Mignonne des rois* (the Favorite of the kings)

---

1. Kingdon, *Myths*, 32.
2. Stjerna, *Women and the Reformation*, 150.

during her childhood. The king had other reasons for showering her with affection, since she was destined to inherit her father's kingdom, and François wanted to avoid a marriage in conflict with the interests of his crown.[3] Both François I and Emperor Charles V schemed to arrange a marriage propitious to their ambitions of annexing Béarn to their territories.

When Jeanne was thirteen, her uncle François pressured her parents into a political marriage for their daughter. He chose to marry his niece to a German prince, Guillaume de La Marck, Duc de Clèves, twelve years her senior, while her parents wanted a marriage either to the *dauphin* of France or the *infant* Phillipe of Spain, son of Charles V.[4] They believed a marriage to the son of Charles V more advantageous to recover Navarre which was partially under Spanish control. Jeanne protested the marriage to La Marck in writing several times. She was perfectly conscious of her actions when she rebelled against the arbitrary authority of her uncle and demonstrated a strong personality at an early age. She allegedly told the king she would rather throw herself into a pit than marry the duke, had to be carried to the altar, and refused to pronounce the sacramental "yes." Given her age, the marriage was not consummated, and documents were gathered for an eventual annulation. The marriage was annulled without any difficulty by Pope Paul III in 1545.[5]

After the death of François I, Jeanne's cousin Henri II came to the throne and arranged a marriage with a *prince du sang* (prince of the blood), Antoine de Bourbon. He was born on April 22, 1518, at La Fère in Picardy between Soissons and Laon, the second son of Charles IV de Bourbon and Françoise d'Alençon. Antoine was a prince of high rank, a direct descendant of Louis IX (r. 1226–70) and in the line of succession to the throne of France behind the son of Henri II. His younger brother, Louis de Bourbon, Prince de Condé, led the Huguenots during the French Wars of Religion. Through this marriage, the House of Navarre was enriched with the Duchy of Vendôme. Jeanne and her husband named their first child Henri de Beaumont, who died tragically at the age of two. She gave birth to the future Henri IV in 1553 at the age of twenty-five, and the child was placed in the care of his grandfather.[6]

---

3. Haag and Haag, *France protestante*, 1:32.
4. D'Aas, *Jeanne III d'Albret*, 79.
5. D'Aas, *Jeanne III d'Albret*, 98.
6. D'Aas, *Jeanne III d'Albret*, 149.

Jeanne and Antoine de Bourbon were crowned Queen and King of Navarre at the death of Henri d'Albret on May 24, 1555.[7] Antoine vacillated between Protestantism and Catholicism, and Jeanne initially hesitated to embrace Reformed teaching. She feared losing her domains through the military might of Henri II. In 1556 Antoine was still among the ranks of faithful Catholics during religious processions, with a candle in hand. When he saw the progress of the Reformation in 1557, he hoped to use it to his advantage. Jeanne hesitated between the Catholic and Reformed religions, attending both the Mass and Protestant services and fearing the vengeance of the kings of France and Spain for the rejection of Catholicism. She initially remained faithful to the Catholic Church in the hope of reform. Her correspondence at the time, however, clearly shows her adherence to Reformed teaching as early as 1555.

Jeanne's public conversion to the Reformed faith and participation in the Lord's Supper took place on Christmas Day in 1560 at Pau. Once convinced of Reformed teachings, she never looked back. In 1568 she wrote of her conversion that "it pleased God by his grace to remove me from the idolatry in which I had sunk and to receive me into his Church."[8] Queen Elizabeth I of England congratulated her on her conversion and encouraged her to propagate the faith. Calvin saw in her conversion important support for the Reformation, especially in light of her husband's commitment to Catholicism. From then on, it was Jeanne and not her husband who Calvin designated for the evangelization of France. Calvin wrote her to express his joy at the news of her conversion and the mercy shown to her by God, who "inscribed the faith of his gospel deep in your heart."[9]

The spectacular conversion of Jeanne, under the influence of Théodore de Bèze, contrasted with the irresolution of her husband, Antoine de Bourbon, and brought a political response to growing calls for repression of the Protestant movement. On her voyage to Paris in 1561 to meet Catherine de Medici, she stopped along the way at Limoges and cities of the Loire Valley, including Tours, and frequented places of worship. Upon her arrival in Paris, fifteen thousand Protestants waited for her with enthusiasm. She was received as a queen with a grand ceremony and fireworks displays and was

---

7. Bayrou, *Henri IV*, 14.
8. D'Aas, *Jeanne III d'Albret*, 256.
9. D'Aas, *Jeanne III d'Albret*, 257.

escorted by her husband and nobles. She intended to make an impression on public opinion and show the strength of her religion.[10]

Antoine opposed the Edict of January of 1562 under Catherine de Medici that provided limited rights for Protestant worship and aligned himself with François de Guise, the instigator of the massacre of Huguenots at Vassy in Champagne in March of that same year. News of the massacre that included women and children was received with enthusiasm in the capital. Upon his return to Paris to join his Catholic allies, Antoine requested that Jeanne leave the Court for Vendôme and refused to allow her son Henri to leave with her. Before leaving, she pleaded with him to remain faithful to the Reformed religion. Jeanne stopped at Meaux on her way to Vendôme and met with her brother-in-law Louis de Bourbon, Prince de Condé. Condé was organizing the Huguenot army after the massacre at Vassy plunged France into the first war of religion. Condé was galvanized by the presence of Jeanne, who participated in the plan to attack Orléans that was captured on April 2.[11] He faced off against his brother Antoine in June near Orléans. The skirmishes ended in the retreat of Condé. Antoine and François de Guise led Catholic forces to retake the cities of Blois, Tours, and Bourges from Protestant control.[12]

During her stay at Vendôme, Jeanne was saddened by the reports from the court that the Reformed religion would not be tolerated in the kingdom. Her time there was marked by the plundering of churches, especially the château of the dukes of Vendôme, the fief of the House of Bourbon-Vendôme. She disarmed the city and allowed her troops to destroy religious images as a means to proclaim the Reformed faith and affirm the transcendence of God. After an inventory of the treasures of Saint-George Collegiate, relics, jewels, precious stones, chandeliers, and statues, the gold and silver were delivered to the Huguenot army for war expenses. Her soldiers desecrated Bourbon sepulchers, and Catholic propaganda used these sacrilegious acts to demonize her. Distraught by these events, Jeanne requested Bèze's advice. He responded that apart from the inexcusable destruction of sepulchers, she had some responsibility for these actions and advised her against recklessness.

When news reached the court of the activities of Jeanne and her troops, Antoine threatened to imprison her, and she left Vendôme for the

---

10. Miquel, *Guerres de religion*, 223–24.
11. D'Aas, *Jeanne III d'Albret*, 293.
12. Stéphan, *Épopée huguenote*, 130.

security of Béarn. While on her journey, Catherine sent Blaise de Monluc to pursue her. She found refuge at Caumont, and over two hundred troops came from Béarn to safely escort her back to Pau. Antoine failed in his attempts to send emissaries to the Bearnaise Parlement to remove all traces of Protestantism. Interreligious conflict continued the following months and during the siege of Rouen in October 1562. Antoine was shot when he imprudently left the trenches to relieve himself. He died from his wounds in November at the age of forty-three, and a rumor circulated that he returned to the Reformed faith before his death.[13]

The year 1562 ended in the shedding of blood. On December 19 the Huguenot army was defeated at Dreux under the command of Louis de Condé, with over six thousand dead and Condé taken prisoner. Jeanne had deliberately abstained from openly entering into the conflict on the side of Condé and Coligny. François de Guise, whom Jeanne held responsible for her husband's betrayal, emerged as the victor and was appointed lieutenant general of the kingdom. His position was cut short when he was assassinated in February 1563 by a Huguenot noble. Coligny was suspected to be behind the assassination, and his enemies would exact their revenge in 1572. Concessions granted by Catherine de Medici with the Edict of Amboise in March 1563 restored peace in France, a peace that satisfied no one.[14]

After Antoine's death, Jeanne demonstrated great courage in daring to reveal to powerful Catholic leaders her commitment to a minority, persecuted religion. As the sovereign of Béarn, Jeanne began to affirm her authority in advancing the Reformed faith as the state religion following the Genevan model. Calvin corresponded with Jeanne and sent Jean-Raymond Merlin to guide her in the offensive against Catholicism. The stronghold of Nérac became an important center for Protestantism in the Midi. Catholic ceremonies and processions were abolished, and statues were removed from plundered churches in Lescar and Pau. Sacred objects were seized or destroyed. The theoretical equality of the two confessions sharing religious edifices was proclaimed in Béarn. In reality, however, Reformed worship triumphed over the Mass and aroused the anger of the Catholic clergy. In October 1563, Jeanne's case was brought before the Holy Office of the Inquisition. She was aware of the terrible anathema pronounced by Pope Julius II (p. 1503–13) against her paternal grandparents, Jean d'Albret and Catherine of Navarre. There was fear that Philippe II would seize Béarn as

---

13. D'Aas, *Jeanne III d'Albret*, 294–97.
14. D'Aas, *Jeanne III d'Albret*, 312.

Ferdinand II had seized Spanish Navarre in 1512.[15] Jeanne found an unlikely ally in Catherine de Medici, alarmed by possible repercussions in France. She did not intend to allow the Vatican to exercise authority over sovereigns or establish a precedent that might affect France in the future.[16]

King Phillipe II of Spain (r. 1556–98) viewed the establishment of Calvinism in Béarn and the diffusion of Protestant literature in his lands as a provocation. He devised a plan for a marriage between his son Carlos or his brother Juan d'Austria to Jeanne. This marriage would offer Phillipe undeniable benefits, bringing Jeanne back to the Catholic Church and reuniting Spanish Navarre, Basse-Navarre, and Béarn. Spain represented a grave danger for Jeanne, something she learned early on from her father and her husband Antoine de Bourbon. Without success, Philippe pressed Jeanne to enforce the decisions of the Council of Trent. She was also warned of inevitable reprisals from the pope and Catholic princes if she did not change her religious policy. Jeanne refused to bend and considered that she had the right to serve God and the gospel in her own lands just as Catholic sovereigns exercised their rights in their own lands.[17]

Jeanne's religious policies did not go uncontested and in 1566 led to riots in Béarn. Lieutenant General Antoine de Gramont, aware of the discontentment of her Béarnaise and Basques subjects, pressured her to soften her stance on religious matters. Her deputies echoed the concerns of local resistance, and a plot against her was foiled in February 1567. A handful of men, animated by a profound repudiation of Protestantism, fomented a plan to kidnap her and her two children. Shortly before the plan's execution, a loyal Catholic discovered the conspiracy and informed Jeanne's former lieutenant general, Armand de Gontaut, who led troops to protect Jeanne. Uprisings continued in several cities before the insurrection ended with the imprisonment of its leaders.[18]

The last years of Jeanne's reign signaled a remarkable period in French religious history. Her leadership and noble status gave hope and needed support to the Huguenot cause. Before the outbreak of the second war of religion in 1567, she obtained permission from Charles IX to take her son Henri de Navarre to visit their domains. To the dismay of Charles IX, Jeanne profited from this voyage to take Henri without permission to

15. D'Aas, *Jeanne III d'Albret*, 327–28.
16. Babelon, *Henri IV*, 126–27.
17. D'Aas, *Jeanne III d'Albret*, 318–21.
18. D'Aas, *Jeanne III d'Albret*, 363–65.

Béarn. At the time of their departure, Louis de Condé and Admiral Gaspard de Coligny left the court as well, and Huguenot leaders took up arms once more.[19] They found refuge at La Rochelle, and the third war of religion broke out. Huguenot forces were defeated at the Battle of Jarnac in March 1569, and Condé was executed when he tried to surrender. Coligny escaped and rejoined Jeanne, who presented her sixteen-year-old son Henri and the fourteen-year-old son of Condé to the troops as their new military leaders.[20]

When the troops of Charles IX were pushed back from the borders of Béarn and Basse Navarre in 1569 by Jeanne d'Albret's army, the king took note of the power of this state dictated by the Protestant identity of the queen and her subjects. French sovereigns were troubled by the geographical proximity of Béarn and the Basse Navarre to their arch-enemy Spain and understood the risk of having its enemies enter the kingdom through these borders. Prospects for peace were heightened in 1572 when Jeanne and Catherine de Medici arranged the marriage of their children, Henri de Navarre and Marguerite de Valois, King Charles IX's sister.

Jeanne did not live to attend her son's August 18 wedding and died a slow and painful death from tuberculosis in June 1572. Both friend and foe agreed that the death of the Queen of Navarre was a great loss for Protestantism. News of her death was received with great relief by ultra-Catholics throughout Europe. The archbishop of Rossano, Italy saw the hand of God in her death.[21] Neither did she live to see the Saint Bartholomew's Day Massacre, which took place on August 24 several days after the wedding. Her ally Coligny was murdered in cold blood, two to three thousand Reformed believers lost their lives in Paris, and thousands more in the provinces fell to the slaughter. Catherine reaffirmed her domination over King Charles IX with the death of Coligny and received the felicitations of the pope. And when she saw her son-in-law, Henri de Navarre, kneel devoutly before the altar at his conversion to Catholicism and promoted Chevalier de Saint-Michel, she boasted that the Huguenots had received a mortal blow. The Saint Bartholomew's Day massacre did not produce its desired effect—to rid the kingdom of schismatic Protestants—and Henri's coerced conversion did not last. After he escaped from the French Court, he continued the Huguenot struggle that his mother had so valiantly led.[22]

19. Babelon, *Henri IV*, 137–38.
20. Stéphan, *Épopée huguenote*, 136–37.
21. D'Aas, *Jeanne III d'Albret*, 507–8.
22. Stéphan, *Épopée huguenote*, 142.

Chapter 13

Louis I de Bourbon, Prince de Condé (1530–69)

Huguenot General

STEPHEN M. DAVIS

LOUIS I DE BOURBON was a descendant of Louis IX (r. 1226–70) and founder of the House of Condé.[1] The Prince de Condé proved his valor as a Huguenot leader during the first three Wars of Religion and died at the Battle of Jarnac in 1569 at the hands of an assassin.[2] One French historian described him as "young, poor, ambitious, eager for pleasure, spiritual and playful, reckless and pugnacious, who espoused the Reformation more by ambition than conviction."[3]

Louis was born in 1530, the youngest son of Charles IV, Duc de Vendôme, and Françoise d'Alençon, and was orphaned at an early age. He grew up under the care of Queen Marguerite de Navarre and was introduced to the Reformed faith through his first wife, Eléanore de Roye, with whom he had eight children. In the service of Henri II (r. 1547–59), he stood out as a remarkable military commander, during which time he converted to Protestantism. Together with François de Guise, he retook Calais

---

1. There was a later Louis II de Bourbon, Prince de Condé (1621–86), known as the "Grand Condé" for his military victories.
2. Haag and Haag, *France protestante*, 1:xxxiii.
3. Stéphan, *Épopée huguenote*, 87.

from the British in 1558 after a two-hundred-year occupation. By 1562 Condé became one of the great Protestant leaders of France. After Eléonore died in 1564, he married Françoise d'Orléans-Longueville, with whom he had three sons. His eldest son, Henri I de Bourbon, became the protector of the United Provinces in the Midi.

On May 13, 1557, four thousand Protestants gathered in Paris to sing psalms at the Pré-aux-Clercs, a vast prairie along the Seine facing the Louvre. Three days later another gathering took place, with Louis de Bourbon and his older brother Antoine de Bourbon present. Positions among the high nobility became clearly established with the all-powerful Guise family on one side and the Bourbons on the other. The House of Guise, an offshoot of the Dukes of Lorraine, had been established in France after the reign of Louis XII (r. 1498–1515) when Claude de Lorraine married Antoinette de Bourbon. The Guises became more influential during the brief marriage between François II and Mary Stuart, Queen of Scots. The Bourbons were *princes du sang* but at a distant degree from the throne and possessing modest wealth. They were also viewed with suspicion since Charles III de Bourbon (1490–1527) plotted with Henry VIII of England and Emperor Charles V to take up arms against King François I. The rivalry for the throne between the Guises and the Bourbons lasted for decades and intensified when the Valois dynasty ended with the assassination of Henri III in 1589. For forty years the Guises were the true heads of the Catholic party, and without them, the Reformed religion might have become dominant in France.[4]

In May 1559, French Calvinists held their first national synod that solidified the Reformation in France. Their Confession of Faith provided an ecclesial structure composed of local assemblies, regional colloquies, provincial synods, and a consistory of twelve elders. A new religious confession was established in France, and the monarchy felt threatened. On June 2, Henri II signed the Edict of Écouen, establishing the burning at the stake for heretics. The king was accidentally wounded the next month during a jousting tournament, died ten days later, and was succeeded by his son François II. Throughout France, Protestantism gained ground. Reformed churches were founded at Saintes, Cognac, Angoulême, Lectoure, Condom, Agen, and Bergerac. Many among the nobility in the Midi converted to the Reformed faith in sufficient numbers to constitute a threat to royal power. Inspired by the Guises, François II signed a decree on September 5, 1559, to destroy houses where Protestants gathered for worship. The courts of Aix

---

4. Félice, *Histoire des protestants*, 88–89.

and Toulouse rigorously applied the law to arrest, banish, execute, or send to the galleys those apprehended. The execution at the stake on December 23, 1559, of Anne Du Bourg, member of the Paris Parlement and follower of Zwingli, shocked public opinion. His execution did more harm to the Catholic cause than the sermons of a hundred preachers.

Several events marked Louis de Bourbon's short and remarkable life. Upon Henri II's death, Catherine de Medici (1519–89) became regent to the young François II, who was under the influence of the Guises through his brief marriage to their niece, Queen Mary Stuart of Scotland. The Guises kept the Bourbons from any influence at the court and published edicts calling for the extermination of the Protestant heretics. Each parlement was instructed to send heretics to the stake through special courts of justice established to deal with heresy (*chambres ardentes*). Protestants in major cities were arrested and their possessions confiscated. Nobles who came to the court to reclaim lost lands were turned away by the Cardinal de Lorraine, brother of François de Guise. Plans were undertaken by Protestant nobles to remove the young king from the influences of the Guises.[5]

Condé waited at Orléans for the outcome as the "silent captain" of the conspiracy.[6] After the conspiracy was unmasked and over fifteen hundred conspirators executed, Condé was called before the king to defend himself. There were indications of collusion between the conspirators and the *princes du sang* but no solid evidence to indict them. Condé was indignant that anyone would suspect him and offered to duel those who accused him. Nonetheless, he was forced to leave the court, and the Guises remained masters of the terrain.[7] The failed conspiracy and the repercussions were harmful to the Protestant cause. From then on, many Catholics considered the Huguenots seditious enemies of the kingdom who needed to be exterminated. Many Protestants, convinced of their loyalty to the crown and persuaded of the justice of their cause, considered the executed conspirators martyrs and sought vengeance.[8]

When the Estates-General was convoked in Orléans on December 10, 1560, the Guises invested the city with thousands of soldiers. The *princes du sang* fell into a trap and were insulted in the streets by soldiers. Condé was arrested, imprisoned, and condemned to death. The prince refused to

5. Félice, *Histoire des protestants*, 99–101.
6. Miquel, *Guerres de religion*, 211.
7. D'Aas, *Jeanne III d'Albret*, 241.
8. Stéphan, *Épopée Huguenote*, 91.

answer Chancellor Michel de L'Hôpital's questions, claiming that L'Hôpital was the henchman of his enemies who wanted him dead, and demanded to be judged by his peers. L'Hôpital intervened to delay carrying out the death sentence against Conde.[9] With young King François II ill, Catherine was hesitant to kill Condé and place herself at the mercy of the Guises. François died on December 5, 1560, Catherine became queen regent, and ten-year-old Charles IX (r. 1560–74) became king. Antoine de Bourbon was appointed lieutenant general of the army, Condé spared, and the enraged Guises chased from power. Catherine was now in the position to maneuver between the Bourbons and the Guises. She lent her support to the Reformation in permitting Admiral Gaspard de Coligny, the Princess de Condé, and nobles to hold prayer meetings in their apartments at Fontainebleau.[10]

Reformed believers joyfully profited from this time of clemency. On the banks of the Loire, they assembled in armed groups. In Languedoc, ministers preached and sang psalms in public places. Military protection was provided by *gentilshommes*[11] for public preaching in Brittanny, Dauphiné, and Provence. Calvin considered these open displays of religious activity a dangerous provocation. From the spring of 1561 to the following year, the Reformed movement aroused indignation among Catholics, distressed at seeing armed parades in the streets of their cities and villages. Protestant fanatics chased priests and the faithful from Catholic churches in Languedoc and Guyenne. In Dauphiné, armed groups led by *gentilshommes* entered churches, breaking images and forbidding Catholics to enter for worship.[12]

The Edict of January in 1562 authorized Reformed worship in limited places. This edict of pacification was unwelcome in many places. In provinces dominated by Protestants, Catholics did not understand the attitude of royal authority toward a competing religion. Now the objects of persecution, Catholics awaited the return of the Guises and met violence with violence, and Protestants were executed for the first time since Catherine de Medici's arrival to power.[13] François de Guise was the instigator of the massacre of Huguenots at worship in Vassy in March 1562, which

---

9. Galand-Willemen and Petris, *Michel de L'Hospital*, 26–27.

10. Stéphan, *Épopée huguenote*, 99.

11. *Gentilshommes* were nobles attached to the person of the king, a prince, or a grand seigneur (*Nouveau Petit Robert*, 1146).

12. Miquel, *Guerres de religion*, 219–22.

13. Miquel, *Guerres de religion*, 226–27.

commenced the first war of religion. The massacre produced an extraordinary impression throughout the kingdom. Reformed believers were filled with indignation and horror. This was not a crime of commoners led by misguided priests. François was a great seigneur of France who slaughtered Protestants, contrary to a royal edict, and received a triumphal entry at Paris.[14] The violence continued. At Tours, a band of Catholics drowned two hundred Huguenots in the Loire. When Condé took control of Orléans with a detachment of horsemen, other cities rallied to him. Protestants held the Loire Valley, Saintonge, Poitou, Dauphiné, the Rhône Valley, major cities in Normandy, Guyenne, and half of Languedoc. Churches were pillaged, priests were attacked, and church bells were melted to make cannonballs. Antoine de Bourbon commanded the king's troops and expelled all Protestants from Paris. Hatred toward him was so great that his family's tombs were desecrated and the remains dispersed.[15]

Condé became isolated at Orléans, abandoned by his officers who returned to their provinces. In desperation, he sought foreign assistance from Elizabeth I of England. Through the Treaty of Hampton in September 1562, she promised her support of money and men in exchange for Le Havre as a pledge and the restitution of Calais after the victory. François de Guise and Antoine de Bourbon were both wounded during the battle to take the city of Rouen. Antoine succumbed to his wounds and Condé became the first *prince du sang* and Catherine de Medici's main rival. Condé prepared to march on Paris but met resistance south of Dreux from royal troops reinforced by German and Swiss troops recruited by Catherine. The Huguenot army engaged in a bloody battle and were severely beaten by the Constable de Montmorency and François de Guise. Condé was wounded and taken prisoner; his army fled in disorder. In place of Antoine de Bourbon, François was rewarded with his appointment as lieutenant general of the kingdom only to be assassinated a few weeks later by Jean Poltrot de Meré at the siege of Orléans.

The edict of pacification of Amboise on March 19, 1563, ended the hostilities. Called a peace of princes, the edict displeased all sides, especially Protestants. They obtained the freedom of worship in one city per district (*bailliage*) but were not permitted to construct new temples. Protestant worship in Paris was forbidden. Nobles were allowed to worship in their homes but only with their families and subjects. Admiral de Coligny

---

14. Félice, *Histoire des protestants*, 151–53.
15. Miquel, *Guerres de religion*, 229–31.

reproached Condé for his part in an edict that favored the nobles, and Calvin accused the princes of vanity and treason. They obtained the freedom of worship for themselves and abandoned the common people, since only nobles were free to convert to Protestantism. Catherine emerged triumphant in finally confining the Reformation to tolerable limits. The principal leaders of the rebellion were dead, aged, or discredited. But with Protestant armies controlling half the kingdom, the struggle was far from over.[16]

Catherine de Medici held fast to the royal tradition that the monarch was the sovereign of all the French. Many French Catholics believed that the riches and fortunes of France were from the hand of God, and military defeats were attributed to the refusal of kings to stamp out heresy. Reformed believers were treated as not truly French, having rejected the religion of the king and through their treasonous alliance with Elizabeth I. Catherine persuaded Condé and Coligny to break with Elizabeth, and with Condé's assistance Protestants and Catholics united behind Catherine to retake Le Havre from the English on July 30, 1563. Flushed with success, Catherine flattered herself in showing the world that a woman could save a kingdom. On August 17, 1563, Charles IX declared his majority, and Catherine undertook the entertainment of the nobility through festivals, banquets, and tournaments. Condé enjoyed the life of the court. He reportedly forgot both his wife and his political allies and was deaf to the reproaches of Calvin, who died on May 27, 1564.[17]

At the worst moments of the religious wars, Protestants claimed allegiance to the king. Their combat was against the Guises and foreign princes, and they feared an alliance between Catherine and Philippe II of Spain (1527-98).[18] Condé withdrew from the court after being publicly insulted by the teenage Duc d'Anjou, the future Henri III, who claimed command of the army as lieutenant general. Coligny was solicited to lead a plot to snatch the young King Charles IX. When the plot was discovered by Catherine, the king was taken to Paris under the protection of Swiss mercenaries. Condé and Coligny sought negotiations with the court and presented their grievances. They requested the dismissal of the Swiss mercenaries, the removal of the Guises from power, and authorization for Protestant worship. To no avail. Skirmishes broke out between royal forces and Condé's troops. Although Italian and Swiss troops reinforced the royal army, Catherine feared

---

16. Miquel, *Guerres de religion*, 234-37.
17. Stéphan, *Épopée huguenote*, 132-33.
18. Miquel, *Guerres de religion*, 247-48.

that they would be no match for the Protestant troops now numbering thirty thousand. Protestant leaders were confident of victory yet worried about how they would feed and pay German mercenaries. Catherine negotiated a truce with Condé at Longjumeau on March 23, 1568, to end the second war of religion. The Treaty of Longjumeau lasted only six months and merely reestablished the Edict of Amboise. Charles IX agreed to pay the Protestant troops and the Swiss mercenaries, conditioned by their immediate withdrawal from the kingdom to avoid further pillaging. The king was humiliated by his forced return to Paris and dreamed of revenge against his Huguenot antagonists. Another war was on the horizon.[19]

Catholics once again were the masters at the court, and Catholic Leagues were formed in the provinces to counter the growing Protestant numbers. The king reneged on his word to dismiss Swiss mercenaries, and the cities under Huguenot control prepared for armed conflict. The Huguenot population at Nîmes slaughtered Catholics and their priests and threw them in wells on September 30, 1567, a massacre known as the Michelade. Condé and Coligny, surveilled by the queen's agents day and night, escaped from Paris on August 23, 1567, and arrived at La Rochelle on September 19. There they found Jeanne d'Albret with her young son, Henri de Navarre, and troops from Gascony. Troops joined them from Brittany and more than twenty thousand recruits from the Midi. The third war of religion broke out in September 1568, and in March 1569 the two armies met face-to-face on the banks of the Charente River at the Battle of Jarnac. Condé was attacked by mercenaries and royal troops and broke his leg falling from his horse. After surrendering to a Catholic *gentilhomme*, he was shot in the head by Captain Montesquiou, an officer of the Duc d'Anjou who paraded Condé's body on a donkey to the laughter of his men. Catholics celebrated the news of Condé's death, and Charles IX sent captured Huguenot banners to the pope.[20] Coligny escaped to La Rochelle, where Jeanne d'Albret presented two new Huguenot leaders, her son Henri and her nephew Henri, the teenage son of Louis de Condé. The Huguenot army had two new *princes du sang* at their head.[21]

From the ambitions and intrigues of three families, the Bourbons, the Guises, and the Montmorency, religious wars bloodied France for three decades. Historians have debated whether the Bourbons caused more harm than good to the image of the French Reformation. They entangled

---

19. Miquel, *Guerres de religion*, 262–64.
20. Félice, *Histoire des protestants*, 180–81.
21. Miquel, *Guerres de religion*, 265–67.

the Reformation in politics, dragged it onto the battlefields, embroiled it in their quarrels, and at times denied the Reformed faith.[22] To his credit, Louis de Condé valiantly defended the Reformed cause. There are doubts about the sincerity of his faith. There is no doubt about his courage and influence in advancing the French Reformation.

---

22. Stéphan, *Épopée huguenote*, 88.

Chapter 14

Antoine de Chandieu (1534–91)
Silver Horn

STEPHEN M. DAVIS

ANTOINE DE CHANDIEU WAS a French theologian who played a decisive role in the religious history of the sixteenth century but remains in the shadow of other French Protestant leaders. Due to his remarkable abilities and his contribution to the Reformation in France, Chandieu has been considered the "Silver Horn," between the better-known John Calvin (Gold) and Théodore de Bèze (Bronze).[1] As pastor of the Reformed Church of Paris almost from its origin, his name became linked to the history of this city's martyrs and the synodal organization of French Protestantism.

Antoine de la Roche was born in Dauphiné, a former province in southeastern France, into an ancient family, the barons of Chandieu. His father died when he was four, and his widowed mother saw to the education of Antoine and his older brother Bertrand, heir of the name and the lordship of Chandieu. Antoine was directed toward formal studies in preparation for a government position, and his brother was destined for military service. Sent to Paris for his education, Antoine was placed in the care of a tutor influenced by the ideas of Calvin and continued his studies in Toulouse, a city marked by religious repression. There his eyes were opened to the errors of the Catholic Church. Despite persecution by the Parlement

---

1. Van Raalte, *Silver Horn*, 6–7. Van Raalte's book is an excellent scholarly source for Chandieu's life and writings.

of Toulouse, reputed as the bloodiest in all of France, the new teachings attracted secret followers and sympathizers. The faithfulness of martyrs was the most powerful form of preaching. The conversion and martyrdom of several respected professors led students to leave their study of law to study the Bible in Geneva.[2]

Antoine was known as Monsieur de la Roche until the death of his brother Bertrand at the Battle of Dreux in 1562, at which time Antoine became the sieur de Chandieu.[3] La Roche left for Geneva and was won to the gospel through Calvin's influence, although the exact date and duration of his stay are unknown. He returned to Paris in 1555, when Reformed believers were organizing a church. The twenty-two-year-old pastor Jean la Maçon, known as La Rivière, was the son of a rich, Catholic royal prosecutor. During his stay in Geneva and Lausanne, La Rivière embraced Reformed teachings and was banished from his parents' home. Soon the church's responsibilities required another pastor. Calvin, Bèze, and Guillaume Farel succeeded in sending François de Morel to collaborate with La Rivière. La Roche was already a part of the church, received training in evangelism and preaching from Morel, and at twenty-two years old was appointed as a pastor with La Rivière. A third pastor, Jean de Lestre, was added in 1557. The three friends, La Rivière, La Roche, and de Lestre, served together in the Paris church for several memorable years. The last years of Henri II (r. 1547–59), the short reign of François II (r. 1559–60), and the beginning of the reign of Charles IX (r. 1560–74) were marked by persecution that was occasionally interrupted by the political fluctuations of Catherine de Medici.[4]

Protestants generally gathered at night in small groups in homes throughout different neighborhoods of the capital for the celebration of worship. In this way, the church was able to meet without arousing suspicion. The church's numerical growth eventually led to a disaster on September 4, 1557, of which La Roche provided a detailed account. Three to four hundred Reformed believers were gathered at night to observe the Lord's Supper in a large home on the rue Saint-Jacques in proximity to the Collège du Plessis. Upon leaving at midnight, the attendees were pelted by stones amassed by the priests from the Collège who had been spying on the assemblies. The noise awakened the entire neighborhood, and armed

---

2. Bernus, *Ministre Antoine de Chandieu*, 3–6.
3. Di Mauro, "Antoine de Chandieu," 219.
4. Bernus, *Ministre Antoine de Chandieu*, 6–8.

citizens blocked the passages of escape. Many inside decided to force their way through the crowd behind sword-bearing *gentilshommes*. Others, mostly women, children, and old men, feared leaving and remained in the besieged house the rest of the night. Come morning, they were arrested and dragged through the enraged mob to the Châtelet and imprisoned. Most of them languished in the dungeons; seven were burned at the stake. Although this event brought great sorrow to the church, the assemblies were not suspended, and the precautions were redoubled in the face of increasing danger.[5]

After the attack at rue Saint-Jacques, La Roche was arrested, along with Jean Morel and de Lestre. La Roche and de Lestre were liberated while Morel remained imprisoned and wasted away for months, subjected to multiple torments. His gentleness and piety led to the conversion of several of his companions in captivity. In February 1559, his life ended in the misery of his dungeon with the suspicion of poisoning and his corpse burned as a heretic. La Roche ended his narrative of the martyrdom of this young man with this beautiful testimony: "It is impossible to recount how much he benefited the Church of God, gifted with God's admirable graces."[6]

At the end of 1560, La Roche was sent by the church of Paris to support and encourage Admiral de Coligny at the convocation of the Estates-General at Orléans. The Protestant cause appeared lost. Coligny's brother François d'Andelot had been imprisoned at Melun for courageously declaring before the king that he did not believe in the Mass. His wife was harassed by priests, and her faith was strengthened by La Roche and de Lestre. Louis de Condé had been arrested and condemned to death, and his brother Antoine de Bourbon, the King of Navarre, was placed in a precarious position. All hope had been dashed by the victorious intrigues of the all-powerful Guises and their influence over the young King François II. The trial of several ministers, including La Roche and La Rivière, was imminent, and the church consecrated the last ten days of November to prayer. The death of François II on December 5, 1560, changed everything, and the Guises lost their grip on power.[7] Catherine de Medici reportedly requested the church of Paris to send La Roche to meet with her out of a desire to receive religious instruction. The consistory sent a memorandum in his place rather than put La Roche's life in danger. Reformed believers

---

5. Bernus, *Ministre Antoine de Chandieu*, 10–12.
6. Bernus, *Ministre Antoine de Chandieu*, 13–14.
7. Bernus, *Ministre Antoine de Chandieu*, 15–16.

enjoyed a respite from persecution as Catherine sought to further weaken the Guises' influence.[8]

Of all the pastors in Paris, Antoine de La Roche was the best known and the most threatened, due to his great abilities and his social status. For his protection, the Consistory of Paris occasionally required him to leave Paris for several weeks at a time when his adversaries were in pursuit. He refused a call to leave France to join the refugees in London and when ministry in Paris became impossible, he served other churches without remuneration. Some historians have seen the hand of La Roche in the Confession of Faith and Discipline of Reformed churches in 1559 at the first national synod and his influence in subsequent synods. He was the author of the *Épître au roi* (*Letter to the King*) that was attached to the Confession of Faith and presented to François II at Chenonceau after the failed Conspiracy of Amboise in 1560. His brother Bertrand was implicated in the plot to kidnap the king, and La Roche, judged guilty by association, was rejected by the Queen Mother as a delegate to the Colloquy of Poissy in 1561.[9]

A time of needed rest for La Roche at his estate in Beaujolais was interrupted by the massacre of Protestants at Vassy in March 1562. The breakout of the first war of religion forced all Reformed pastors to leave Paris when Huguenots were expelled in May. Pastors, elders, and many other Protestants found refuge at Orléans, a bulwark of the Reformed army. With the city under siege and ravaged by plague, La Roche and his colleague La Rivière ministered for a year, with an important influence on seventy-two other ministers who had found refuge there. La Roche took the lead in the name of Reformed churches in opposing Louis de Condé during negotiations for the Peace of Amboise in 1563.

The imprisoned Louis de Condé negotiated with Catherine de Medici under pressure to end his captivity and sold out Reformed interests. The treaty was ratified without the assent of Coligny and became a source of discouragement for Reformed believers, with limitations on places of worship. La Roche wrote in his journal that Reformed churches felt abandoned and in a worse state than before the war. The sixth article of the treaty forbidding Reformed worship in Paris effectively exiled La Roche and La Rivière from their Paris church. La Rivière withdrew to Angers, his native city, and served the church until he fell at the hand of assassins following the Saint Bartholomew's Day massacre in August 1572. In 1563, La Roche

---

8. Bernus, *Ministre Antoine de Chandieu*, 19.
9. Bernus, *Ministre Antoine de Chandieu*, 24–28.

published his *Histoire des persécutions et martyrs de l'Eglise de Paris depuis l'an 1557 jusques au temps du roy Charles neuvième* (*History of Persecutions and Martyrs of the Church in Paris from 1557 to the Time of King Charles IX*). Reformed believers were permitted to return to Paris but without their pastors. In September the church was reestablished as well as the circumstances allowed. Believers gathered secretly in small groups throughout Paris although La Roche was too well known to return.[10]

At the death of his brother at the Battle of Dreux in December 1562, La Roche became the head of his family and was addressed as Monsieur de Chandieu. Neither his new title nor his fortune changed anything in his simple lifestyle. He remained committed to his pastoral calling and the work of God. In the aftermath of his exile from Paris following the Peace of Amboise, he entered into possession of the Château de Pôle. La Rivière and de Lestre were present as witnesses of his marriage contract on May 30, 1563. The wedding was celebrated the following month with Françoise de Felin of the family of the lords of Banthelu, a family devoted to the Reformed cause. Françoise was associated with the difficult life of Chandieu for twenty-eight years as a faithful companion. She shared his faith, his hopes, and his sorrows; carried the burden of concern for the dangers he faced; had a great part in the education of their children; and was at his side when he closed his eyes for the last time in the land of his exile.[11]

Protestants grew bolder, even in the face of opposition from the parlement. Marshal de Montmorency, Governor of Paris, firmly maintained order and repressed all acts of violence. A provincial synod meeting at La Ferté in 1564, with thirty-eight ministers and sixty elders under the presidency of Chandieu, demonstrated the vigor of reorganized churches in the Paris region, Picardy, and Brie. The fifth national synod met secretly in Paris in 1565, although it is not known if Chandieu was present. His care for the church of which he remained pastor was through letters, prayer, and stealthy visits. Finally, in June 1567 he received authorization from the consistory to return to his ministry with prudence. Yet three months later, at the beginning of the second war of religion, he was forced to withdraw once again from Paris. He would never return to the capital.[12]

Chandieu labored in Bourgogne to reorganize and establish churches in places authorized by the Peace of Amboise. He consecrated his time and

---

10. Bernus, *Ministre Antoine de Chandieu*, 29–33.
11. Bernus, *Ministre Antoine de Chandieu*, 37–41.
12. Bernus, *Ministre Antoine de Chandieu*, 34–35.

strength to the church of Lyon, a large congregation that had remained in Protestant hands during the first war of religion. Of the three Protestant temples in Lyon built to replace those taken from them, one was demolished in 1566 before its completion, and the two others suffered the same fate the next year at the beginning of the second war of religion in 1567. Protestants were expelled from the city, their possessions were confiscated, and any remaining Protestants who refused to convert to Catholicism were imprisoned. The church of Lyon was dissolved, and the waters of the Rhône carried the bodies of those massacred. Pastors were especially pursued, and Geneva again received refugees who were cared for with funds from Protestant lands. The Peace of Longjumeau in March 1568 ending the second war of religion provided no relief with its unfulfilled promises. The king forbade Protestant worship in Lyon, and in flagrant violation of the edict's provisions, religious prisoners were not released, and confiscated possessions were not returned to their owners.[13]

Chandieu fled his home in August 1568 after several attempts on his life and wandered for nine days with his antagonists in pursuit. He crossed the Saône River at midnight, made his way to Geneva, found the city ravaged by a plague, and went on to Lausanne before returning to Geneva. One month after his flight, the king forbade the practice of the Reformed religion, and the third war of religion began. Chandieu's wife was forced to remain in France to avoid the confiscation of their properties. She visited him twice and on the second visit gave birth to their fifth child, Suzanne, who was left in the care of her father.[14] In February 1570 he received news that his family was in danger and his château was occupied by the enemy. It was during this period that he composed the *Ode sur les misères des Églises françaises* (*Ode on the Miseries of French Churches*). He painted a moving portrait of the cruelties with which Protestants were afflicted and ended with the prayer "that all may with the same courage worship the only Living God."[15]

After years of desolation came a period of peace with the Treaty of Saint-Germain in August 1570, which brought to an end the third war of religion and accorded limited freedom of worship for Protestants. Chandieu returned to France and his family and participated in two national synods with Théodore de Bèze in La Rochelle and Nîmes. The brief respite was broken on August 24, 1572, with the Saint Bartholomew's Day Massacre.

13. Bernus, *Ministre Antoine de Chandieu*, 43–44.
14. Bernus, *Ministre Antoine de Chandieu*, 48–49.
15. Bernus, *Ministre Antoine de Chandieu*, 52–56.

The carnage began in Paris and continued in the provinces. Like thousands of others, Chandieu once again took the route of exile, this time for eleven years.[16]

Once in Geneva, "Chandieu's name was inscribed on the register of the Company of Pastors."[17] His next ten years were spent in relative tranquility and the education of his children. Two of his children died before the massacre and four fled with their parents. Six more children were born in exile, two of whom died shortly after birth, and their last child was born and died after their return to France. The Academy of Lausanne invited him to the position of professor of theology in 1577. Two years later a plague ravaged Lausanne, forcing Chandieu and his family to leave for Aubonne, between Lausanne and Geneva, where he remained until July 1583. During this period of calm, he composed several of his writings. He translated his *Méditations sur le Psaume XXXII* (*Meditations on Psalm 32*) from Latin into French and dedicated it to the Protestants of France who had been forced to enter the Catholic Church.[18]

The Treaty of Fleix in November 1580 ended the seventh war of religion and brought order and security to France. Chandieu left Aubonne for his home country in 1583 to visit his land holdings and establish himself at Pôle.[19] In September 1584 he was a delegate to a Reformed assembly permitted by Henri III (r. 1574–89) at Montauban and returned home to devote himself to his theological writings. The year 1584 began a new era of troubles that plunged France into another civil war. At the death of Henri III's younger brother, François, Duc d' Anjou (1555–84), Henri de Navarre became the first in line to the throne. The Guises allied themselves with Spain and presented their own candidate for royal succession. In June, Chandieu left for Geneva for the safety of his family and returned alone to Pôle.[20]

For three years Chandieu served as chaplain to Henri de Navarre and was one of the pastors who prayed before the Battle of Coutras in October 1587. The battle ended in a great victory for the Huguenots, and Chandieu proclaimed the humiliation of the prince's enemies, whose banners lined the victor's walls.[21] Chandieu's health suffered from life in military

16. Bernus, *Ministre Antoine de Chandieu*, 58.
17. Manetsch, *Calvin's Company of Pastors*, 58.
18. Bernus, *Ministre Antoine de Chandieu*, 79–80, 84–85.
19. Bernus, *Ministre Antoine de Chandieu*, 93.
20. Bernus, *Ministre Antoine de Chandieu*, 109–110.
21. Babelon, *Henri IV*, 385–87.

camps, and he fell gravely ill at Nérac in November 1587. Once recovered he was permitted to join his family the following spring in Geneva after a three-year separation. Fifteen days later he was charged with missions to the cantons of Reformed Switzerland and the Protestant princes of Germany. He returned to Geneva in May 1588 and was charged by Navarre to receive funds from Switzerland and Germany to pay debts incurred for the maintenance of the king's troops. With the assassination of Henri III in 1589, Navarre was designated his successor. Chandieu received his first letter from King Henri IV in January 1590 and continued correspondence with him. Despite the king's weaknesses, Chandieu retained a profound affection for him. He did not live to see Henri IV convert to Catholicism in 1593.[22]

In his last years, Chandieu served the church in Geneva without remuneration, continued his theological writing, and corresponded with pastors in France. Along with Bèze, his advice and opinions were sought for questions of doctrine and church discipline. Amid this activity, God suddenly called his servant home on February 23, 1591.[23] As his death approached, Chandieu consoled his family and exhorted them to remain strong in the Lord. He passed into eternity in peace, and a great silence took hold of the city, such was the sorrow. No one grieved more than Bèze, who had seen in the younger Chandieu his successor.[24]

The social position of Antoine de Chandieu's family had promised him a brilliant future with wealth and honors. He sacrificed it all for the ministry of the gospel, with its attendant dangers of suffering and exile, and left a legacy for Reformed churches that reverberates to the present day. After his death, his writings in Latin were collected and reprinted multiple times as a testament to his reputation as an esteemed theologian.

---

22. Bernus, *Ministre Antoine de Chandieu*, 115–16.

23. Chandieu's son Daniel gave this date for his father's death (Bernus, *Ministre Antoine de Chandieu*, 127). Others have suggested he died in March 1591 (Manetsch, *Calvin's Company of Pastors*, 58).

24. Bernus, *Ministre Antoine de Chandieu*, 123–26.

Chapter 15

Henri IV (1553–1610)
First Bourbon King

STEPHEN M. DAVIS

HENRI DE NAVARRE BECAME the nominal ruler of France after the assassination of Henri III of France (r. 1574–89), whose marriage to Louise de Lorraine produced no heir. After years of attempts to deny the throne to Navarre, his enemies realized they could not defeat him militarily. The French Wars of Religion had exhausted the country, and it became clear that Henri would need to adopt the religion of the majority of his subjects to assure the freedom of conscience for Protestants with whom he had a religious affinity and who had fought by his side.

Henri de Navarre, son of Antoine de Bourbon and Jeanne d'Albret, was born at the Château of Pau in Béarn on December 13, 1553. Even before his birth, Henri was the object of a battle for influence. His father Antoine de Bourbon, wanted him to be born in La Flèche, a territory belonging to the Bourbons; his grandfather Henri d'Albret, King of Navarre, insisted his birth take place in Pau.[1] His baptism into the Catholic religion took place early in 1554 with King Henri II (r. 1547–59) as his godfather, represented by Cardinal de Bourbon. At this time his mother Jeanne, fearing the loss of her domains, had not openly made a profession of the Reformed religion. After he was weaned, Henri was entrusted to a governess, Suzanne

1. Bayrou, *Henri IV*, 24–26.

de Bourbon-Busset, a cousin of the Albret family. She was told to raise him *à la béarnaise*, that is, austerely, never calling him prince and dispensing corporal punishment as needed. Young Henri lived in Coarraze in the province of Béarn with occasional visits to the Royal Court. In February 1557, Antoine and Jeanne traveled to the court to officially present their young heir.[2]

From the age of eight to ten, Henri remained at the court under the influence of Catherine de Medici and shared his life with the royal children. Charles IX, three years older than him, became king in 1560 upon the death of his brother François II. Another childhood companion was the future King Henri III who was successively titled Duke of Angoulême, Duke of Orléans, and Duke of Anjou. A third companion was François d'Alençon, a year younger than Henri, named Hercules at his birth. In reality, he was sickly and small in stature, and his early death prevented him from becoming king. Henri II and Catherine de Medici's daughter Marguerite was the same age as Henri and destined to become his future wife. Court life opened up his knowledge of the world as he mastered social codes and reinforced his capacity for dissimulation. Despite his real friendships with the royal children, he experienced a period of familial isolation and solitude.[3]

Henri was still a child during the early days of the Reformed movement's rapid growth in the early 1560s and the violent precursors to the Wars of Religion. He had been torn between Catholicism and the Reformed faith through the influence of his parents. Henri's father Antoine vacillated between Catholicism and Protestantism for political reasons. On Christmas Day 1560, his mother Jeanne publicly affirmed her conversion to the Reformed faith. Henri returned to the court in 1561 with his mother when Catherine organized the Colloquy of Poissy to provide the occasion for Catholic and Protestant theologians for public debate in a failed attempt to reconcile the two religions.

On January 17, 1562, Catherine de Medici issued the Edict of January. Huguenots were granted limited rights for private religious practices in government-approved places. The authorities of the Catholic Church considered Catherine's edict in contradiction to the Council of Trent, and war seemed inevitable. The massacre of Huguenots in Vassy on March 1, 1562, foreshadowed the bloodshed that followed in the Wars of Religion for over

---

2. Babelon, *Henri IV*, 52.
3. Bayrou, *Henri IV*, 69.

three decades. These wars "made clear that France was divided—regionally, socially, and politically—by Calvinism."[4]

Henri's father Antoine was wounded during the siege of Rouen in 1562 and died shortly after. Following his death, Catherine de Medici wanted Henri raised at the court but left educational decisions to his mother, Jeanne d'Albret. Almost overnight, the child left the Mass for the Lord's Supper, and his Catholic teachers were dismissed.[5] After the first war of religion, Catherine organized a vast voyage throughout the kingdom from 1564 to 1566 to save the kingdom from civil war. King Charles IX had reached his majority, and it was time to further his education of the kingdom and show his military power. Along with the king in the procession were his brothers Henri and François, his sister Marguerite and his mother, and the young Henri de Navarre.[6]

Henri undertook his first military campaign in February 1568 to put down an insurrection led by nobles in the territories of his mother. He was at his mother's side at Cognac in September of that year and showed remarkable poise when the city opened its gates to him as head of the House of Bourbon. At Angoulême he assisted at his first siege and was catapulted to the leadership of the Huguenot resistance at the age of fifteen after the death of Louis de Condé at the Battle of Jarnac in 1569. He distinguished himself in combat for the first time at the battle of Arnay-le-Duc in June 1570, when he took command of the opening charge, leading to a great Huguenot victory. The peace of Saint-Germain-en-Laye followed in July, ending the third war of religion and providing, among other provisions, four Huguenot strongholds: La Rochelle, Montauban, La Charité, and Cognac.[7]

After the third war of religion, Catherine de Medici drew closer to Reformed leaders and arranged a marriage between her daughter Marguerite de Valois (1553–1615) and Navarre, whose mother Jeanne died two months before the marriage. The ceremony took place with great pomp on August 18, 1572. Four days later, on August 22, an attempt was made on the life of Admiral Gaspard de Coligny, who was thought responsible for the murder of François de Guise in 1563. Early in the morning of August 24, 1572, a small band of assassins led by the Duke of Guise headed to the inn where Coligny was recovering from his wounds. Soldiers posted by Charles IX

---

4. McGrath, *Life of John Calvin*, 193.
5. Babelon, *Henri IV*, 105–07.
6. Babelon, *Henri IV*, 122–23.
7. Babelon, *Henri IV*, 147–58.

for Coligny's protection joined the band, murdered Coligny in cold blood, and threw his lifeless body out a window. Three days of massacre followed in Paris where two to three thousand Reformed believers lost their lives. As the news from Paris spread to the provinces, the Catholic populations of many cities set upon the Protestants to exterminate them. Both Henri de Condé and Henri de Navarre abjured Protestantism to save their lives.[8]

Once freed from the court, Navarre publicly revoked his abjuration, took his place at the head of Huguenot forces and engaged in skirmishes with small contingents of armed forces. The Battle of Coutras on October 20, 1587, was the first major battle for the King of Navarre. Henri allied himself with his Catholic cousins of the House of Bourbon—François de Bourbon, Prince de Conti; and Charles de Bourbon, Count of Soissons—to present a united dynastic front against the Guises. The royal army led by Duke Anne de Joyeuse was defeated, and de Joyeuse was killed in battle along with his brother Claude de Saint-Sauveur. Navarre returned the bodies to the families and attended a Mass in honor of the deceased enemies.[9]

Navarre had been raised in the Reformed faith by his mother after her public confession of faith in 1560. Under his father's influence, he returned to Catholicism in 1562 and back to the Reformed confession after his father's death that same year. When Henri III outlawed the Reformed religion in July 1585, Navarre's succession to the crown was invalidated. Pope Sixtus V declared Navarre a heretic and excommunicated him. During the years 1588 and 1589, Navarre multiplied military activity in Normandy and around Paris. After Henri III's rupture with the Catholic League and his complicity in the assassination of Henri de Guise in 1588, he drew closer to Navarre. Henri III was assassinated in August 1589 at the hands of the Dominican monk Jacques Clément. Before his death, Henri III implored Navarre to convert to Catholicism and recognized Henri de Navarre as his successor.[10]

Navarre took command of his troops, now composed of Protestants and Catholics, defeated the Duke of Mayenne at Arques in September 1589, and besieged a resistant Paris. In March 1590, the famous Battle of Ivry and Navarre's decisive victory opened the way for a new siege of Paris against the city's militias. A complete blockade of the city worsened living conditions and led to widespread famine and illness. Only the intervention of Spanish troops forced the lifting of the siege in September. Although

8. Babelon, *Henri IV*, 183–90.
9. Babelon, *Henri IV*, 379.
10. Petitfils, *Assassinat d'Henri IV*, 43–44.

Navarre had great military successes early on, the failed siege at Paris broke his élan.[11] After decades of war, France was exhausted. The nation was in a desperate condition, and there seemed no end to the struggles. Yet Navarre knew that as a Huguenot he would never be accepted as king by the majority of the French people.

Modern historians have generally lauded Henri IV for sacrificing his religious scruples in adopting the religion of the majority of French people to end the interminable civil wars. One historian describes him as "cynical" but nonetheless "saved France from religious discord."[12] On July 25, 1593, Navarre solemnly recanted in the Basilica of Saint-Denis leading to his coronation as King Henri IV of France at the Cathedral of Chartres on February 27, 1594. His abjuration was attacked as feigned by some preachers in Paris, yet many citizens simply wanted peace and a united nation free from foreign influence. The cities of Paris, Rouen, Meaux, Poitiers, and many others accepted Henri IV's conversion with conditions that included banning Protestants from gathering in their cities. Huguenots were permitted to worship throughout the kingdom, even discreetly at the court, and army officials celebrated the Lord's Supper in the camps. With these conditions, the Protestants provisionally maintained their confidence in Henri IV.[13]

Even after Henri IV's coronation, there were excesses of religious intolerance. In 1595 an estimated two hundred Huguenots worshiping at Châtaigneraie in Vendée were massacred. In response to the continuing violence, the king promulgated an edict of pacification, the Edict of Nantes on April 13, 1598. The edict imposed religious coexistence and was met with resistance by Catholics and Protestants. Rome continued to oppose any change in the Catholic Church's privileged position in France.[14] After years of religious wars, the edict did not immediately extinguish all the grudges and resentment. However, it opened a new period in relations between Catholics and Protestants and provided relative security and tolerance for the Huguenots. The Treaty of Vervins, signed in May between Henri IV and Philippe II of Spain, brought a temporary entente between the two nations and contributed to Henri IV's rising stature in the affirmation of his power and the stability of his reign.[15]

11. Miquel, *Guerres de religion*, 374.
12. Davies, *Europe*, 539.
13. Félice, *Histoire des protestants*, 251.
14. Babelon, *Henri IV*, 680–84.
15. Babelon, *Henri IV*, 623–24.

The Edict of Nantes was Henri IV's crowning achievement in its imposition of religious coexistence. Protestants did not obtain full religious freedom, and Protestant worship was authorized only in places where it existed in 1597. Protestants were not allowed missionary activity to open new places of worship, while Catholics opened churches in places where Catholicism had virtually disappeared. Royal texts until this time had referred to Protestantism as the new religion (*nouvelle religion*). In the preamble to the Edict of Nantes, Protestants now belonged to the So-Called Reformed Religion (*Religion Prétendue Réformée*), with the king's wish that these subjects return to the true religion, now his own.

Henri IV survived multiple plots and assassination attempts before falling at the hand of a Catholic zealot, Jean-François Ravaillac, on May 14, 1610. On that May afternoon, the king took his place in his royal carriage, leaving the Louvre accompanied by his *gentilshommes*. Paris was preparing to celebrate with pomp the official entry of Marie de Medici after her coronation the previous evening in Saint-Denis. While the carriage was blocked by the congestion of carts, Ravaillac jumped onto the carriage and stabbed the monarch three times. The assassin was seized and quartered before a hysterical crowd. Questions remain unanswered to this day. Was this the work of someone mentally unbalanced? Was it an isolated act by a disenchanted religious fanatic who, even under torture, refused to implicate anyone else? Was it directly the work of the Catholic League, whose influences drove him to regicide?

The ignominious death of Henri IV remains one of the great enigmas of the history of France and among the most important and tragic events of modern times. One can only imagine what might have been accomplished if he had lived longer and the kingdom had been spared the disaster of Marie de Medici's unpopular regency. In Europe, the relations between the major powers would have changed. The assassination arrived at a time to serve the interests of the Habsburgs, who ruled in Vienna, Madrid, Brussels, and Naples. If Henri IV had not been killed on May 14, a few days later he would have joined his troops gathered in Champagne in a campaign against Spain and the German emperor. Certainly, Philippe III of Spain, Emperor Rudolph II, and Albert and Isabelle, co-souverains of the Spanish Netherlands, had reason to want Henri removed from power. France had reconstituted its military forces during ten years of peace following the ravages of the Wars of Religion. Henri IV's death permitted the

Habsburgs to continue their domination. Were they complicit? Perhaps we will never know for sure.[16]

Henri IV remains one of the great paradoxes of French Protestantism, a man who changed religions several times during his life. With his death, the Protestant cause lost its greatest protector, and his murder strengthened an absolute monarchy. The crime of *lèse-majesté* reinforced the will to elevate kings to a sacred and inviolable place and supported the doctrine of *droit divin*. The throne was placed so high that to disobey the king was tantamount to disobeying God. The smallest threat to kings became an obsession in the seventeenth and eighteenth centuries and brought ruthless repression.[17] To his credit, Henri IV lifted his weary nation out of over thirty years of civil war. Yet his refusal to create a parliamentary monarchy as protection from future abuses of power led his son Louis XIII to undermine the Edict of Nantes. His grandson, Louis XIV, revoked the edict in 1685, and Protestants once again entered the furnace of persecution.

---

16. Petitfils, *Assassinat d'Henri IV*, 9–12.
17. Petitfils, *Assassinat d'Henri IV*, 276.

Conclusion

The first ten years of the seventeenth century following the Edict of Nantes marked a Catholic renewal, with concessions designed to prevent further warfare. The edict authorized the complete institutional restoration of the Catholic Church in every corner of the kingdom, even in places where the majority of inhabitants had converted to the Reformed faith. Protestants needed to prepare for the return of priests, who had been absent for two generations.[1] Catholic processions resumed in places where there had been none for decades. Tensions were often high in cities with two places of worship, two cemeteries, two categories of the king's subjects, and even two church bells.[2]

The edict was enforced during the reign of Henri IV, at times with great difficulty, until his assassination. His death alarmed the Protestant community that feared the loss of its acquired rights. Following her husband's death, Marie de Medici (1575–1642), the second wife of Henri IV, became queen regent from 1610 to 1617 during the minority of their son Louis XIII (r. 1610–43). She confirmed the Edict of Nantes in a declaration on May 22, 1610, but Protestants had little confidence in her.[3]

Protestants retained territorial possession of strongholds in more than one hundred cities in France, including La Rochelle, Saumur, Montpellier, and Montauban. During this period of tolerance, these cities became semi-autonomous states within the kingdom. They held political assemblies, developed territorial organizations, maintained military fortresses, and practiced diplomacy and relations with foreign powers, notably England.

1. Birnstiel, "Conversion des protestants," 95–96.
2. Miquel, *Guerres de religion*, 409.
3. Stéphan, *Épopée huguenote*, 206–8.

CONCLUSION

La Rochelle became the principal bastion of the Reformed religion and was supported by England, which sought to curb the development and expansion of the French navy.[4] The presence of Protestant strongholds became intolerable for Louis XIII. Marie de Medici succeeded in introducing Armand du Plessis de Richelieu (1585–1642) into the court of Louis XIII in 1624. Louis XIII and Richelieu sought to force the submission of Protestants to royal authority and reinforce the unity of the kingdom. The city of La Rochelle stood as a formidable barrier to their designs and had become the principal stronghold of the Huguenot party.[5]

Cardinal Richelieu did not hide his intention to establish the absolute authority of the king on the ruins of La Rochelle. The city had been besieged several times during the sixteenth-century Wars of Religion without success. Admiral Gaspard de Coligny, Jeanne d'Albret, and Henri de Navarre had found refuge behind her walls. La Rochelle was the most secure and well-armed city of the French Reformation.[6] In 1627, La Rochelle was besieged for a year and cut off from all outside provision, and Richelieu ordered the construction of an enormous dike to prevent any help from the sea. La Rochelle capitulated on October 28, 1628 and Louis XIII entered La Rochelle on November 1 to receive its surrender. He abolished all the former benefits the city enjoyed, ordered most of the ramparts leveled, and turned the Protestant temples over to the Catholic Church. After years of sacrifice, La Rochelle's destiny was now tied to the French monarchy and the Catholic Church.[7]

In a matter of only a few years, the Protestant situation in France radically and perilously reversed. Louis XIV (r. 1643–1715) unleashed the ferocious *dragonnades*, which constrained Protestants to lodge the king's troops to force conversions to Catholicism. Catholic clergy persuaded the king that the success of these measures had diminished the Reformed religion through conversion or emigration to the point where few Protestants were left in France. Louis XIV finally yielded to the clergy's pressure to obtain the Revocation of the Edict of Nantes on October 18, 1685, also known as the Edict of Fontainebleau. The king's subjects were compelled to adopt the religion of the king. The Revocation of the Edict of Nantes offered a façade of unity. Through state violence, France falsely believed the kingdom

---

4. Lacava and Guicharnaud, *Édit de Nantes*, 3.
5. Delumeau, *Christianisme*, 97.
6. Félice, *Histoire des protestants*, 296.
7. Stéphan, *Épopée huguenote*, 214–15.

had rediscovered national and spiritual unity. One hundred years later, the French monarchy and the French clergy paid dearly for their tyranny. The victors of the Revocation became the victims of the Revolution. Louis XVI and his family were massacred by their subjects. Priests were forced into exile and found refuge among the descendants of those whom their predecessors had persecuted.[8]

After the Reformed religion was outlawed by the Revocation of the Edict of Nantes, Protestant temples were destroyed, and pastors were exiled. The War of the Camisards (1702–4) was launched by Protestant Huguenots in the Cévennes region of southern France.[9] The court at Versailles learned that Holland and England were in contact with the insurgents and had promised them support. Louis XIV sent Field Marshal de Villars to negotiate with the insurgents with assurances of limited freedoms. The Camisard leader Jean Cavalier surrendered. He and one hundred of his men were escorted by the king's soldiers from the kingdom, never to return. The remaining Camisards were demoralized, their days marked by dissension, hunger, fear, and despair. Sensing the cause lost, the Camisard leaders surrendered one by one, and they were permitted to leave France for Switzerland.[10]

Louis XIV issued a declaration in March 1715 stating that all subjects of the king were also subjects of the Catholic Church. Anyone who declared that he or she wanted to live and die in the Reformed religion, whether they recanted or not, was considered Catholic, and the refusal of the sacraments exposed them to punishment.[11] Toward the end of Louis XIV's reign, the hostility of the Catholic Church to new converts and the shame of those who made insincere conversions "combined to produce the materials with which the French Protestant Church could be rebuilt."[12] In defiance of the king's decree, Antoine Court (1696–1760) gathered a small group of believers to lay new foundations for Reformed churches in France. The Church of the Desert entered a new phase in 1715 under the leadership of Antoine Court. He considered four conditions necessary for the reorganization of Reformed churches: regular public gatherings, the disavowal of the disorder caused by those claiming the Holy Spirit's inspiration, the establishment of

8. Cabanel, "Enchanter, désenchanter," 414–15.
9. See Davis, *War of the Camisards*, for an account of the war.
10. Crété, *Camisards*, 243–44.
11. Félice, *Histoire des protestants*, 424–25.
12. Poland, *French Protestantism*, 31.

CONCLUSION

church order through consistories and synods, and rigorous training for pastors. The execution of this plan was accompanied by great difficulties.[13]

The years 1715 to 1760 became known as the "heroic period" of the Church of the Desert, when Protestant gatherings were forbidden and those arrested were severely punished. In 1729, Court left France permanently to find refuge at Lausanne. There he founded a seminary in 1730, which he directed until his death in 1760. Through his writings, he continued defending Protestants from accusations of treason against the monarchy.[14] Only in 1787, with the Edict of Toleration, would French Protestants be considered fully French, with the right to marry before a civil official, register the birth of their children, and bury their dead. Full recognition for Protestants as truly and legally French would come only with the much-maligned French Revolution in 1789.[15]

We conclude here at this point in French history, recognizing the contribution of well-known and lesser-known individuals who sought to return the church to the apostolic teachings of justification by faith alone and the supreme authority of Scripture.[16] Through many dangers, toils, and snares, Protestant Christianity has survived in France to the present day.

---

13. Félice, *Histoire des protestants*, 429.
14. Bost, *Histoire des protestants*, 168.
15. Villepin, *Cent-Jours*, 11.
16. See Davis, *French Protestantism's Struggle* for an account of the period following the French Revolution.

Chronology

1492	Birth of Marguerite de Angoulême (de Navarre)
1515	Death of Louis XII
1515–47	Reign of François I
1516	Guillaume Briçonnet appointed bishop of Meaux
1517	Luther's Ninety-Five Theses
1519	Charles V becomes emperor of Germany
	Erasmus's Greek-Latin *Novum Testamentum*
	Birth of Catherine de Medici
1521	Lefèvre d'Étaples in Meaux
1521	Sorbonne condemns Luther's writings; Luther excommunicated
1523	Jean Vallière burned at the stake
1524	Farel arrives in Switzerland
1526	Treaty of Madrid
1528	Council of Sens condemns heretics at Meaux
	Birth of Jeanne d'Albret (November 16)
1529	Execution of humanist Louis de Berquin
	Treaty of Cambrai between François I and Charles V
1530	Confession of Augsburg (Lutheran)
1533	Marriage of Dauphin Henri de France with Catherine de Medici

CHRONOLOGY

1534	*Affaire des Placards*; Calvin flees France for Switzerland
	Foundation of the Company of Jesus (Jesuits) by Ignace de Loyola
1536	Calvin's *Institutes of the Christian Religion* in Latin; Calvin arrives in Geneva
1541	*Institutes of the Christian Religion* in French
1545	Council of Trent
	Jeanne-d'Albret's marriage to the Duke of Clèves annulled
1546	Death of Luther
1547	Death of François I; death of Henry VIII (England)
1547–59	Reign of Henri II
1548	Marriage of Jeanne D'Albret to Antoine de Bourbon (Oct 20)
1549	Death of Marguerite de Navarre (Dec 21)
1553	Birth of Henri de Navarre (Dec 13)
1555	First Reformed churches in France
1558	Death of Emperor Charles V
1559	Death of Henri II in a jousting accident; François II becomes king
	Coronation of Elizabeth I (England)
	Execution of Anne du Bourg, member of Parlement of Paris
1559	First National Synod of Reformed Churches
	Treaty of Cateau-Cambrésis
1560	Conspiracy of Amboise
	Death of François II
	Conversion of Jeanne d'Albret to Reformed faith (December 25)
1560–74	Reign of Charles IX; Catherine de Medici appointed regent
1561	Colloquy of Poissy
1562	Edict of January (Saint-Germain)
	Massacre of Protestants at Vassy (March 1)
	Beginning of Wars of Religion

CHRONOLOGY

	Death of Antoine de Bourbon (November 17)
	Defeat of the Huguenots at Dreux (December 19)
1563	Edict of Amboise ends first war of religion
	Murder of François de Guise
	Excommunication of Jeanne d'Albret
	End of Council of Trent
1564	Death of Calvin (May 27)
1567	Second war of religion (April 1567–March 1568)
1568	Edict of Longjumeau ends the second war of religion
	Third war of religion (August 1568–August 1570)
1569	Protestants defeated in battles of Jarnac and Moncontour
	Death of Louis de Condé at Jarnac (March 13)
	Restoration of Reformed religion in Béarn
1570	Peace of Saint-Germain ends third war of religion
	Marriage of Charles IX to Elizabeth of Austria
1571	National Synod and Confession of Faith of La Rochelle
1572	Death of Jeanne d'Albret (June 9)
	Marriage of Henri de Navarre to Marguerite de Valois (August 18)
	Saint Bartholomew's Day Massacre (August 24)
1573	Edict of Boulogne ends fourth war of religion
1574	Death of Charles IX
1574–89	Reign of Henri III
1576	Edict of Beaulieu ends fifth war of religion
	Henri de Navarre escapes from the Court
1577	Treaty of Bergerac ends sixth war of religion
1580	Treaty of Fleix ends seventh war of religion
1584	Death of Henri III's brother, Duke of Alençon
	Henri de Navarre becomes heir presumptive to the throne
1585	Edict of Nemours renounces all previous edicts of pacification

CHRONOLOGY

1587	Battle of Coutras
1588	Henri III takes refuge at Chartres
	Assassination of Henri de Guise
1589	Death of Catherine de Medici
	Henri III and Henri de Navarre reconciled
	Assassination of Henri III
	Henri de Navarre (Henri IV) becomes nominal ruler of France
1593	Abjuration of Henri IV at Saint-Denis (July 25)
1594	Coronation of Henri IV at Chartres (Feb 27)
	Jesuits expelled from kingdom
1595	Henri IV receives papal absolution
1597	Amiens taken by the Spanish then retaken by Henri IV
1598	Edict of Nantes ends eighth war of religion (April 13)
1600	Marriage of Henri IV to Marie de Medici (December 17)
1610	Coronation of Marie de Medici (May 13)
	Assassination of Henri IV (May 14)
1610–43	Reign of Louis XIII
1628	Fall of La Rochelle
1643–1715	Reign of Louis XIV
1681	*Dragonnades* unleashed to force Protestant conversions to Catholicism
1685	Revocation of the Edict of Nantes (Edict of Fontainebleau)
1702–4	War of the Camisards
1715	Antoine Court and Church of the Desert
1715–74	Reign of Louis XV
1774–92	Reign of Louis XVI
1787	Edict of Toleration
1789	French Revolution

From the Same Authors

STEPHEN M. DAVIS

Crossing Cultures: Preparing Strangers for Ministry in Strange Places. Eugene, OR: Wipf &Stock, 2019.
"France's Long March from State Religion to Secular State." In *The Palgrave Handbook of Religion and State Volume II: Global Perspectives,* edited by Shannon Holzer, 127–50. Cham, Switzerland: Palgrave-Macmillan, 2023.
The French Huguenots and Wars of Religion: Three Centuries of Violence for Freedom of Conscience. Eugene, OR: Wipf & Stock, 2021.
French Protestantism's Struggle for Survival and Legitimacy, 1517–1905. Eugene, OR: Wipf & Stock, 2023.
God's Unchanging Word in an Ever-changing World: Messages of Hope for Weary Christians. Eugene, OR: Wipf & Stock, 2022.
Missiological Reflections on Life and Mission. Eugene, OR: Wipf & Stock, 2022.
Rise of French Laïcité: French Secularism from the Reformation to the Twenty-First Century. Eugene, OR: Pickwick, 2020.
Urban Church Planting: Journey into a World of Depravity, Density, and Diversity. Eugene, OR: Resource Publications, 2019.
The War of the Camisards (1702–1704): Huguenot Insurrection during the Reign of Louis XIV. Eugene, OR: Wipf & Stock, 2024.

MARTIN I. KLAUBER

90 Days with the Christian Classics. With Michael Bauman and Keith Wells. Nashville: Broadman & Holman, 2000.
The Great Commission: Evangelicals and the History of World Missions. Edited with Scott Manetsch. Nashville: Broadman & Holman, 2008.
Historians of the Christian Tradition: Their Methods and Impact on Western Thought. Edited with Michael Bauman. Nashville: Broadman & Holman, 1995.
The Identity of Geneva: The Christian Commonwealth, 1564–1864. Edited with John B. Roney. Westport, CT: Greenwood, 1998.
Pastoral Care in the Protestant Tradition. Edited with Jeff Fisher. Eugene, OR: Wipf & Stock (forthcoming).

FROM THE SAME AUTHORS

The Synod of Dort: Historical, Theological, and Experiential Perspectives. Contributor and co-editor with Joel Beeke. Göttingen, DE: Vandenhoeck & Ruprecht, 2020.

The Theology of the Early French Reform: From the Affair of the Placards to the Edict of Nantes. Editor and contributor. Grand Rapids: Reformation Heritage, 2023.

The Theology of the French Reformed Churches: From Henry IV to the Revocation of the Edict of Nantes. Editor and contributor. Grand Rapids: Reformation Heritage, 2014.

The Theology of the French Reformed Churches: From the Revocation of the Edict of Nantes to the Edict of Toleration. Editor and contributor. Grand Rapids: Reformation Heritage, 2020.

Bibliography

Amphoux, Henri. *Michel de L'Hôpital et la liberté de conscience au XVIe siècle.* Geneva: Slatkine, 1969.
Babelon, Jean-Pierre. *Henri IV.* Paris: Fayard, 1982.
———. "Henri IV et la réforme." *Bulletin de la Société de l'Histoire du Protestantisme Français* 156 (2010) 595–606. http://www.jstor.org/stable/24310105.
Bainton, Roland H. *Hunted Heretic: The Life and Death of Michael Servetus, 1511-1553.* Boston: Beacon, 1960.
———. *Women of the Reformation in France and England.* Minneapolis: Augsburg, 1973.
Barker, S. K. *Protestantism, Poetry and Protest: The Vernacular Writings of Antoine de Chandieu (c. 1534-1591).* London: Routledge, 2009.
Barnaud, Jean. *Pierre Viret: Sa vie and son œuvre (1511-1571).* Saint-Amans: G. Carayol, 1911.
Barzun, Jacques. *From Dawn to Decadence: 1500 to the Present.* New York: Harper Collins, 2000.
Bayrou, François. *Henri IV.* Paris: Éditions Flammarion, 1998.
Bellius, Martin. *De Haereticis, an Sint Perseqvendi, et omnino quomodo sit cum eis agendum, Doctorum uirorum tum ueterum, tum recentiorum sententiae.* Argentorati: Johannis Caroli, 1610.
Benedict, Philip. *Christ's Churches Purely Reformed: A Social History of Calvinism.* New Haven: Yale University Press, 2002.
———. "The St. Bartholomew's Day Massacre in the Provinces." *Historical Journal* 2 (1978) 205–25.
Bernus, Auguste. *Le ministre Antoine de Chandieu: D'après son journal autographe inédit (1534-1591).* Paris: Imprimeries Réunies, 1889.
Beuzart, Paul. "Sur l'origine de Louis de Berquin." *Bulletin de la Société de l'Histoire du protestantisme français* 87 (January–March 1938) 45–49.
Bevan, Frances. *Vie de Guillaume Farel.* 1885. Reprint. Phoenix: Éditions Théotex, 2012.
Bèze, Théodore de. *Confession de la foy chrestienne.* Geneva: Jacques du Pan, 1563. https://tinyurl.com/BezaConfession.
———. *Un grand de l'Europe.* Translated by Jean-Louis Dumas. Paris: Bergers Mages, 2000.
———. *Histoire ecclésiastique des églises reformées au royaume de France.* Vol. 1. Lille: Imprimerie de Leleux, 1841.

———. *The Life of John Calvin*. Translated by Henry Beveridge. Philadelphia: Westminster, 1909.

Birnstiel, Eckart. "La conversion des protestants sous le régime de l'Édit de Nantes (1598-1685)." In *Religions, pouvoir et violence*, edited by Patrick Cabanel and Michel Bertrand, 93-113. Toulouse: Presses Universitaires du Midi, 2004.

Borello, Céline. *Catherine de Médicis*. Paris: Presses Universitaires de France, 2021.

Bost, Charles. *Histoire des protestants de France*. 9th ed. Carrières-sous-Poissy, FR: Éditions La Cause, 1996.

Bost, Hubert, and Claude Lauriol. *Entre désert et Europe, le pasteur Antoine Court (1695-1760)*. Paris: Honoré Champion, 1998.

Brown, Christopher Boyd. "Calvin and Luther." In *John Calvin in Context*, edited by R. Ward Holder, 299-309. Cambridge: Cambridge University Press, 2020.

Bruening, Michael W. *Calvinism's First Battleground: Conflict and Reform in the Pays De Vaud, 1528-1559*. Dordrecht: Springer, 2005.

———. "Pierre Viret, Reformer on the Margins." In *The Theology of Early French Protestantism: From the Affair of the Placards to the Edict of Nantes*, edited by Martin I. Klauber, 333-56. Grand Rapids: Reformation Heritage, 2023.

———. *Refusing to Kiss the Slipper: Opposition to Calvinism in the Francophone Reformation*. Oxford: Oxford University Press, 2021.

Buchanan, Catherine. "The Massacre of St. Bartholomew's (24-27 August 1572) and the Sack of Antwerp (4-7 November 1576): Print and Political Responses in Elizabethan England." PhD diss., London School of Economics, 2011.

Buchon, J. A. C. *Choix de chroniques et mémoires sur l'histoire de France, avec notices biographiques*. Paris: A. Desrez, 1836.

Buisson, Albert. *Michel de L'Hôpital, 1503-1573*. Paris: Hachette, 1950.

Cabanel, Patrick. "Enchanter, désenchanter l'histoire du Refuge huguenot." *Revue d'histoire du protestantisme* (2017) 409-20. https://www.jstor.org/stable/44850967.

———. *Histoire des protestants en France, XVIe-XXIe siècle*. Paris: Fayard, 2012.

Calvin, John. *Commentaries on the Epistles to Timothy, Titus, and Philemon*. Translated by William Pringle. Edinburgh: Calvin Translation Society, 1856.

———. *Commentary on the Book of Psalms*. Translated by James Anderson. Grand Rapids: Eerdmans, 1948.

———. *Institutes of the Christian Religion*. 1536 ed. Translated by Ford Lewis Battles. Grand Rapids: Eerdmans, 1986.

———. *L'Institution chrétienne (IV)*. 1555. Reprint. Chicago: Éditions Kerygma, 1978.

———. *Ioannis Calvini Opera quae supersunt omnia*, edited by Guilielmus Baum, Eduardus Cunitz, and Eduardus Reuss. 59 vols. Brunsvigae: Schwetschke et filium, 1863-1900.

———. *Letters of John Calvin*, edited by Jules Bonnet. Translated by David Constable. Philadelphia: Presbyterian, 1858.

———. *Letters of John Calvin*. Vol. 3. Translated by Marcus Robert Gilchrist. Philadelphia: Presbyterian, 1858.

———. *A Reformation Debate: John Calvin and Jacopo Sadoleto*, edited by John Olin. 1966. Reprint. Grand Rapids: Baker, 1976.

Cameron, Richard M. "The Charges of Lutheranism Brought Against Jacques Lefèvre d'Étaples (1520-1529)." *Harvard Theological Review* 63 (Jan. 1970) 119-49.

Carroll, Stuart. *Martyrs and Murderers: The Guise Family and the Making of Europe*. Oxford: Oxford University Press, 2009.

BIBLIOGRAPHY

———. *Noble Power During the French Wars of Religion: The Guise Affinity and the Catholic Cause in Normandy*. Cambridge: Cambridge University Press, 1998.

Carayon, H. J. B. L. *Guillaume Farel: Sa vie–Son œuvre*. Toulouse: Bonnal et Gibrac, 1809.

Carroll, Stuart. *Martyrs and Murderers: The Guise Family and the Making of Europe*. Oxford: Oxford University Press, 2009.

Castellio, Sebastian. *Dialogi sacri, latino-gallici, ad linguas, moresque puerorum formandos*. Geneva: Jean Girard, 1543.

Chandieu, Antoine de la Roche. *Histoire des persécutions et martyrs de l'église de Paris: Depuis l'an 1557, jusques au temps du roy Charles neuvième*. Lyon: N.p., 1563. https://gallica.bnf.fr/ark:/12148/bpt6k791047/f4.item.r=antoine%20de%20chandieu.

Chareyre, Philip. "L'Héritage de Pierre Viret en Béarn." In *Pierre Viret et la diffusion de la réforme: Pensée, action, contextes religieux*, edited by Karin Crousaz and Daniela Solfaroli Camillocci, 371–405. Lausanne: Éditions Antipodes, 2014.

Cholakian, Patricia F., and Rouben C. Cholakian. *Marguerite of Navarre: Mother of the Renaissance*. New York: Columbia University Press, 2006.

Chung-Kim, Esther. *Inventing Authority: The Use of the Church Fathers in Reformation Debates over the Eucharist*. Waco, TX: Baylor University Press, 2011.

Cottret, Bernard. *Historie de la Réforme Protestante, XVIe–XVIIIe siècle*. Paris: Perrin, 2010.

Crété, Liliane. *Les Camisards*. Paris: Éditions Perrin, 2007.

Crouzet, Denis. *Dieu en ses royaumes: Une histoire des guerres de religion*. Seyssel, FR: Éditions Champ Vallon, 2008.

———. *Les guerriers de Dieu: La violence au temps des troubles de religion vers 1525–vers 1610*. 2 vols. Seyssel, FR: Éditions Champ Vallon, 1990.

———. *La nuit de la Saint-Barthélemy: Un rêve perdu de la Renaissance*. Paris: Fayard, 1994.

———. *La sagesse et le malheur: Michel de l'Hospital, Chancelier de France*. Seyssel, FR: Éditions Champ Vallon, 1998.

D'Aas, Bernard Berdou. *Jeanne III d'Albret: Chronique (1528-1572)*. Anglet, FR: Éditions Atlantica, 2002.

Daireaux, Luc. "Louis XIV et les protestants normands: Autour de la révocation de l'édit de Nantes." *Bulletin de la Société de l'Histoire du Protestantisme Français* 158 (Jan.–Mar. 2012) 123–32. https://www.jstor.org/stable/24310203.

Daussy, Hugues. *Le parti Huguenot: Chronique d'une désillusion (1557-1572)*. Geneva: Droz, 2015.

D'Aubigné, J. H. Merle. *Histoire de la Réformation du seizième siècle*. Vol. 1. Paris: Librairie Ch. Meyrueis et Compagnie, 1860. https://gallica.bnf.fr/ark:/12148/bpt6k24389r.

Davies, Norman. *Europe: A History*. Oxford: Oxford University Press, 1996.

Davis, Stephen M. *The French Huguenots and Wars of Religion: Three Centuries of Resistance for Freedom of Conscience*. Eugene, OR. Wipf & Stock, 2021.

———. *French Protestantism's Struggle for Survival and Legitimacy (1517-1905)*. Eugene, OR: Wipf & Stock, 2023.

———. *The War of the Camisards (1702-1704): Huguenot Insurrection during the Reign of Louis XIV*. Eugene, OR: Wipf & Stock, 2024.

Delumeau, Jean. *Le christianisme va-t-il mourir?* Paris: Hachette, 1977.

Dennison, James T. *Reformed Confessions of the 16th and 17th Centuries in English Translation (1523-1552)*. Vol. 1. Grand Rapids: Reformation Heritage, 2008.

Diefendorf, Barbara B. *Beneath the Cross: Catholics and Huguenots in Sixteenth-Century Paris*. New York: Oxford University Press, 1991.

———. "Prologue to a Massacre: Popular Unrest in Paris, 1557–1572." *American Historical Review* 5 (Dec. 1985), 1067–91. https://www.jstor.org/stable/1859659.

Di Mauro, Damon. "Antoine de Chandieu, auteur d'un drame biblique?" *Bulletin de la Société de l'Histoire du Protestantisme Français* 151 (2005): 219–29. http://www.jstor.org/stable/24309144.

Doumergue, Émile. "Le vrai chant du vrai psaume huguenot." Valence-sur-Rhône, FR: Imprimeries Réunies, 1929.

Ducasse, André. *Henri IV*. Paris: Fayard, 1982.

Duley-Haour, Pauline. *Mémoires pour servir à l'histoire et à la vie d'Antoine Court*. Paris: Les Éditions de Paris, 2020.

Elton, G. R. *Reformation Europe: 1517–1559*. 2nd ed. Malden, MA: Blackwell, 1999.

Félice, Guillaume de. *Histoire des protestants de France: 1521–1787*. Vols. 1–4. 1880. Reprint. Phoenix: Éditions Théotex, 2020.

Fisher, Jeff. *A Christoscopic Reading of Scripture: Johannes Oecolampadius on Hebrews*. Göttingen: Vandenhoeck & Ruprecht, 2016.

Galand-Hallyn, Perrine. "La *Praelectio in Suetonium* de Nicholas Bérault (1515)." *Humanistica Lovaniensia* 46 (1997) 62–93.

Galand-Willemen, Perrine, and Loris Petris. *Michel De L'Hospital: Chancelier-Poète*. Geneva: Librairie Droz, 2020.

Ganoczy, Alexandre. *The Young Calvin*. Translated by David Foxgrover and Wade Provo. Philadelphia: Westminster, 1987.

Garside, Charles Jr. "'La Farce des Theologastres': Humanism, Heresy, and the Sorbonne." *Rice University Studies* (Fall 1974) 45–82.

Garrisson, Janine, ed. *Histoire des protestants en France: De la Réforme à la Révolution*. 2nd ed. Toulouse: Éditions Privat, 2001.

———. *Henri IV*. Paris: Le Seuil, 2008.

Gordon, Bruce. *Calvin*. New Haven: Yale University Press, 2009.

Graves, Frank P. *Peter Ramus and the Educational Reformation of the Sixteenth Century*. New York: Macmillan, 1912.

Gray, Janet G. "Origin of the Word Huguenot." *Sixteenth Century Journal* 14 (Fall 1983) 349–59.

Greengrass, Mark. *France in the Age of Henri IV: The Struggle for Stability*. 2nd ed. New York: Longman, 1995.

Guessard, M. F. *Mémoires et lettres de Marguerite de Valois*. Paris: Société de l'Histoire de France, 1842. https://gallica.bnf.fr/ark:/12148/bpt6k36525r.

Haag, Eugène, and Émile Haag. *La France protestante, ou vies des protestants français qui se sont fait un nom dans l'histoire*. Vol. 1. Paris: Cros, 1846. https://books.google.com/books?id=63UaAAAAYAAJ.

———. *La France protestante: ou vies des protestants français qui se sont fait un nom dans l'histoire*. Vol. 6. Geneva: Cherbuliez, 1856. https://gallica.bnf.fr/ark:/12148/bpt6k58521008/f325.

Haldane, Charlotte. *Queen of Hearts: Marguerite of Valois*. Indianapolis: Bobbs-Merrill, 1968.

Hamon, Léo, ed. *Un siècle et demi d'histoire protestante: Théodore de Bèze et les protestants sujets du roi*. Paris: Éditions de la Maison des sciences de l'homme, 1989.

Hauréau, Barthélemy. "Louis de Berquin: 1523–1529." *Revue des deux mondes* 79 (Jan. 15, 1869) 454–81.

BIBLIOGRAPHY

Higman, Francis. "La Dispute de Lausanne: Carrefour de la Réformation française." In *La dispute de Lausanne: La théologie réformée après Zwingli et avant Calvin*, edited by Eric Junod, 26–35. Lausanne: Bibliothèque Historique Vaudoise, 1988.

Holt, Mack P. *The French Wars of Religion, 1562–1629*. 2nd ed. Cambridge: Cambridge University Press, 2005.

———. *The Duke of Anjou and the Politique Struggle During the Wars of Religion*. Cambridge: Cambridge University Press, 1986.

Holtrop, Philip C. *The Bolsec Controversy on Predestination, from 1551 to 1555: The statements of Jerome Bolsec, and the Responses of John Calvin, Theodore Beza, and other Reformed Theologians*. Lewiston, NY: Edwin Mellen, 1993.

Hughes, Philip Edgcumbe. *Lefèvre: Pioneer of Ecclesiastical Renewal in France*. Grand Rapids: Eerdmans, 1984.

Jenkins, Gary W. *Calvin's Tormentors: Understanding the Conflicts That Shaped the Reformer*. Grand Rapids: Baker Academic, 2018.

Joblin, Alain. *Louis de Berquin: De l'humanisme au bûcher*. Paris: Éditions Ampelos, 2023.

Jouanna, Arlette. *The Saint Bartholomew's Day Massacre: The Mysteries of a Crime of State*. Translated by Joseph Bergin. Manchester: Manchester University Press, 2007.

Kelley, Donald R. *The Beginning of Ideology: Consciousness and Society in the French Reformation*. Cambridge: Cambridge University Press, 1981.

Kim, Seong-Hak. "'Dieu nous garde de la messe du chancelier': The Religious Belief and Political Opinion of Michel de L'Hôpital." *Sixteenth Century Journal* 24 (Fall 1993) 595–620.

———. *Michel de l'Hôpital: The Vision of a Reformist Chancellor During the French Religious Wars*. Sixteenth Century Essays and Studies. Kirksville, MO: Truman State University Press. 1994.

Kingdon, Robert M. *Geneva and the Coming of the Wars of Religion in France 1555–1563*. Geneva: Librairie Droz, 2007.

———. *Geneva and the Consolidation of the French Protestant Movement, 1564–1572*. Geneva: Droz, 1967.

———. *Myths About the St. Bartholomew's Day Massacres, 1572–1576*. Cambridge: Harvard University Press, 1988.

Knecht, Robert J. *The French Religious Wars, 1562–1598*. Oxford: Osprey, 2002.

———. *Hero or Tyrant?: Henry III, King of France, 1574–89*. New York: Routledge, 2014.

Lacava, Marie-José, and Robert Guicharnaud, eds. *L'Édit de Nantes: Sûreté et Education*. Montauban, FR: Société Montalbanaise d'Étude et de Recherche sur le Protestantisme, 1999.

La Place, Pierre de. *Commentaires de l'estat de la religion et république sous les rois Henry & François seconds, & Charles neuvième*. N.p.: N.p., 1565.

———. *Du droict usage de la philosophie morale avec la doctrine chrestienne*. Paris: Morel, 1562.

———. *The Right Use of Moral Philosophy*. Translated by Albert Gootjes. Grand Rapids: CLP Academic, 2022.

———. *Traitté de la vocation et manière de vivre*. Paris: Morel, 1561.

———. *Traicté de l'excellence de l'homme chrestien et manière de le cognoistre*. Geneva: Jacob Stoer, 1575.

La Tour, P. Imbart de. *Les origines de la Réforme*. Vol. 4. Paris: Firmin-Didot Editeurs, 1935. https://gallica.bnf.fr/ark:/12148/bpt6k5803418x/f1.

Linder, Robert. *The Political Ideas of Pierre Viret*. Geneva: Droz, 1964.

Maag, Karin. *Seminary or University: The Genevan Academy and Reformed Higher Education, 1560–1620*. Aldershot, UK: Scolar, 1995.

Machelon, Jean-Pierre. *La laïcité demain: Exclure ou rassembler?* Paris: CNRS Éditions, 2012.

Manetsch, Scott M. *Calvin's Company of Pastors: Pastoral Care and the Emerging Reformed Church, 1536–1609*. Oxford Studies in Historical Theology. New York: Oxford University Press, 2013.

———. *Theodore Beza and the Quest for Peace in France, 1572-1598*. Leiden, NE: Brill, 2000.

Manetsch, Scott M., and Kirk Summers, eds. *Theodore Beza at 500: New Perspectives on an Old Reformer*. Göttingen: Vandenhoeck and Ruprecht, 2020.

Mann, Margaret. "Louis de Berquin: Traducteur d'Érasme." *Revue du seizième siècle* 18 (1931) 309–23.

McGrath, Alister E. *A Life of John Calvin: A Study in the Shaping of Western Culture*. Oxford: Blackwell, 1990.

McKim, Donald K. "The Function of Ramism in William Perkins' Theology." *Sixteenth-Century Journal* 16 (1985) 503–17.

———. "Peter Ramus in History and Theology." In *The Theology of Early French Protestantism: From the Affair of the Placards to the Edict of Nantes*, edited by Martin I. Klauber, 229–55. Grand Rapids: Reformation Heritage, 2023.

———. *Ramism in William Perkins' Theology*. New York: Peter Lang, 1987.

Mehl, Roger. *Antoine de Chandieu: A Study in the Development of French Protestantism*. Grand Rapids: Eerdmans, 1967.

Metzger, Bruce, and Bart Ehrman. *The Text of the New Testament: Its Transmission, Corruption, and Restoration*. 4th ed. Oxford: Oxford University Press, 2005.

Miller, Perry. *The New England Mind: The Seventeenth Century*. 1939. Reprint. Eastford, CT: Martino, 2014.

Miquel, Pierre. *Les guerres de religion*. Paris: Fayard, 1980.

Mullett, Michael A. *John Calvin*. London: Routledge, 2011.

Murphy, James J., ed. *Arguments in Rhetoric Against Quintilian: Translation and Text of Peter Ramus's Rhetoricae Distinctionis in Quintilianum (1549)*. Translated by Carole Newlands. Carbondale: Southern Illinois University Press, 1986.

Naphy, William G. *Calvin and the Consolidation of the Genevan Reformation*. Manchester: Manchester University Press, 1994.

Le Nouveau Petit Robert de la Langue Française. Paris: Le Robert, 2007.

Nugent, Donald. *Ecumenism in the Age of the Reformation: The Colloquy of Poissy*. Cambridge: Harvard University Press, 1974.

Ong, Walter J. *Ramus, Method, and the Decay of Dialogue*. Cambridge: Harvard University Press, 1958.

Panetta, Odile. "Heresy and Authority in the Thought of Théodore de Bèze." *Renaissance and Reformation* 45 (2022) 33–72. https://www.jstor.org/stable/27206453.

Parker, T. H. L. *Calvin: A Biography*. Louisville: Westminster, 1975.

———. *Calvin's Preaching*. Louisville: Westminster, 1992.

Pédérzet, J. *Cinquante ans de souvenirs religieux et ecclésiastiques*. Paris: Librairie Fischbacher, 1896.

Peña, Santiago Francesco. "A French 'Confessionalization of Humanism'? French Humanists and the Early Reformation." *Archiv für Reformationsgeschichte* 114 (Nov. 2023) 7–32.

Petitfils, Jean-Christian. *L'assassinat d'Henri IV: Mystères d'un Crime*. Paris: Perrin 2009.

———. *Henri IV*. Paris: Perrin, 2021.
Pitts, Vincent J. *Henri IV of France: His Reign and Age*. Baltimore: Johns Hopkins University Press, 2009.
Poland, Burdette C. *French Protestantism and the French Revolution: A Study in Church and State, Thought and Religion, 1685-1815*. Princeton, NJ: Princeton University Press, 1957.
Pouilly, Louis-Jean Levesque de. *Vie de Michel de L'Hôpital, Chancelier de France*. London: David Wilson, 1764. https://archive.org/details/viedemicheldeloolv.
Quackenbos, David C. "Calling in Conflict: John Calvin's Pastoral Theology During His Strasbourg Exile, 1538-1541." *Journal of the Evangelical Theological Society* 65 (Jun. 2022) 333-48.
Ramus, Peter. *Arguments in Rhetoric Against Quintilian: Translation and Text of Peter Ramus's Rhetoricae Distinctionis in Quintilianum (1549)*. Edited by James J. Murphy. Translated by Carole Newlands. Carbondale: Southern Illinois University Press, 1986.
Rentet, Thierry. *Anne de Montmorency: Grand Maître de François Ier*. Rennes, FR: Presses Universitaires de Rennes, 2011.
Roelker, Nancy L. *One King, One Faith: The Parlement of Paris and the Reformations of the Sixteenth Century*. Berkeley: University of California Press, 1996.
———. *Queen of Navarre: Jeanne D'Albret 1528-1572*. Cambridge: Harvard University Press, 1968.
Roney, John B., and Martin I. Klauber, eds. *The Identity of Geneva: The Christian Commonwealth (1564-1864)*. Westport, CT: Greenwood, 1998.
Roussel, Bernard. "Pierre Viret en France (Sep. 1561-Aug. 1565)." *Bulletin de la Société de l'histoire du protestantisme français* 144 (Oct.-Dec. 1998) 803-39. https://www.jstor.org/stable/43497420.
Ryan, P. F. William. *Queen Jeanne of Navarre*. London: Hutchinson, 1911. https://babel.hathitrust.org/cgi/pt?id=njp.32101066227966&seq=21.
Salmon, J. H. M. *Society in Crisis: France in the Sixteenth Century*. New York: St. Martin's, 1975.
Scrivner, F. H. A., ed. *The New Testament in Greek: According to the Text Followed in the Authorised Version Together with the Variations Adopted in the Revised Version*. Cambridge: Cambridge University Press, 1908.
Selderhuis, Herman J. *John Calvin: A Pilgrim's Life*. Downers Grove, IL: InterVarsity, 2009.
Selles, Otto. *Antoine Court: Le patriote français et impartial*. Paris: Honoré Champion, 2002.
———. "The First Sermon of Antoine Court (1695-1760)." In *The Theology of the Huguenot Refuge: From the Revocation of the Edict of Nantes to the Edict of Versailles*, edited by Martin I. Klauber, 257-82. Grand Rapids: Reformation Heritage 2020.
Schaff, Philip, ed. *The Creeds of Christendom with a History and Critical Note*. 6th ed. Revised by David S. Schaff. 3 vols. Grand Rapids: Baker. 2007.
Sharratt, Peter. "Ramus 2000." *Rhetorica* 18 (Fall 2000) 399-455.
Shimizu, J. *Conflict of Loyalties: Politics and Religion in the Career of Gaspard de Coligny, Admiral of France, 1519-1572*. Geneva: Droz, 1970.
Shumaker, Thomas E. "Refuge, Resistance, and Rebellion: Humanism and the Middle Way in the French Wars of Religion." PhD diss., University of New Mexico, 2017. https://digitalrepository.unm.edu/hist_etds/176.
Skalnik, James V. *Ramus and Reform: University and Church at the End of the Renaissance*. Kirksville, MO: Truman State University Press, 2002.
Stéphan, Raoul. *L'Épopée huguenote*. Paris: La Colombe, 1945.

Stephenson, Barbara. *The Power and Patronage of Marguerite de Navarre*. New York: Routledge, 2004.

Stjerna, Kirsi. *Women and the Reformation*. Malden, MA: Blackwell, 2009.

Thysell, Carol. *The Pleasure of Discernment: Marguerite de Navarre as Theologian*. Oxford: Oxford University Press, 2000.

Tipson, Baird. "Seeing the World Through Ramist Eyes: The Richardsonian Ramism of Thomas Hooker and Samuel Stone." *Seventeenth Century* 28 (2013) 275–92.

Treasure, Geoffrey. *The Huguenots*. New Haven: Yale University Press, 2013.

Vance, Jacob. *Secrets: Humanism, Mysticism, and Evangelism in Erasmus of Rotterdam, Bishop Guillaume Briçonnet, and Marguerite de Navarre*. Leiden, NE: Brill, 2014.

VanDoodewaard, Rebecca. *Reformation Women: Sixteenth-Century Figures Who Shaped Christianity's Rebirth*. Grand Rapids: Reformation Heritage, 2017.

Van Raalte, Theodore G. *Antoine de Chandieu: The Silver Horn of Geneva's Reformed Triumvirate*. New York: Oxford University Press, 2018.

Villepin, Dominique de. *Les Cent-Jours ou l'esprit du sacrifice*. Paris: Éditions France Loisirs, 2001.

Vray, Nicole. *Jeanne D'Albret et Henri IV, mère et fils reine de Navarre et roi de France: L'ambiguïté et la foi*. Lyon: Éditions Olivétan 2012.

Waddington, Charles. *Ramus: Pierre de la Ramée, sa vies, ses écrits et ses opinions*. Paris: Ch. Meyrueis, 1855.

Watt, Jeffrey R. "Consistories and Discipline." In *John Calvin in Context*, edited by R. Ward Holder, 103–10. Cambridge: Cambridge University Press, 2020.

Watt, Jeffrey R., and Isabella Watt, eds. *Registres du Consistoire de Genève au temps de Calvin*. Geneva: Droz, 1996–2018.

Weben, Violaine. *Théodore de Bèze: Un grand de l'Europe*. Translated by Jean-Louis Dumas. Paris: Bergers Mages, 2000.

Weiss, Nathanaël. "Louis de Berquin, son premier procès et sa rétractation, d'après quelques documents inédits." *Bibliothèque de la Société de l'Histoire du Protestantisme Français* 67 (1918) 180–81.

White, Henry. *The Massacre of St. Bartholomew: Preceded by a History of the Religious Wars in the Reign of Charles IX*. New York: Harper & Brothers, 1868.

Whitehead, A. W. *Gaspard de Coligny, Admiral of France*. London: Methuen, 1904.

Wilson, Katharina M., ed. *Women Writers of the Renaissance and Reformation*. Athens, GA: University of Georgia Press, 1987.

Wolfe, Michael. "The Conversion of Henri IV and the Origins of Bourbon Absolutism." *Historical Reflections* 14 (1987) 287–309. http://www.jstor.org/stable/41298881.

———. *The Conversion of Henri IV: Politics, Power, and Religious Belief in Early Modern France*. Cambridge: Harvard University Press, 1993.

Wursten, Dick. *Clément Marot and Religion: A Reassessment in the Light of His Psalm Paraphrases*. Leiden, NE: Brill, 2010.

Yardeni, Myriam. *Minorités et mentalités religieuses en Europe moderne: L'exemple des huguenots*. Paris: Honoré Champion, 2018.

Zuidema, Jason. *Guillaume Farel*. Trois-Rivières, QC, Canada: Publications Chrétiennes, 2015.

———. *William Farel*. Darlington, UK: Evangelical Press, 2014.

———, and Theodore Van Raalte. *Early French Reform: The Theology and Spirituality of Guillaume Farel*. London: Routledge, 2011.

Index

Academy of Geneva, 5, 49, 68, 86
Academy of Lausanne, 67, 85, 124
Affair of the Placards, ix, 21, 40, 52, 59
Albret, Jeanne d', viii, 37, 40, 69, 84, 90, 101, **103-9**, 116, 126, 128, 134
Amboise (Conspiracy of), ix, 2, 8, 44, 79, 94-95, 121
Andrea Alciati, 49
Anjou, Henri d'. *See* Henri III.
Anne de Montmorency, 7-8, 77, 95
Anne, Duke of Joyeuse, 129
Antoine Court, 135

Ballay, Guillaume du, 28,
Barry, Jean du, 7, 45, 79, 94
Basel, 5, 21, 25, 27, 50, 52, 59-61, 67
Basilica of Saint-Denis, 130
Battle of Coutras, 124, 129
Battle of Jarnac, 80, 109-10, 116, 128
Battle of Moncontour, 139
Battle of Pavia, 34, 39, 93
Bédier; Noël (Béda), 34-36, 65
Bérault, Nicole, 32-33
Berquin, Louis de, 1-2, **31-36**
Bèze, Théodore de, vii, 5-6, 9, 36, 46, 59, 63, 74-75, **84-92**, 95, 98-99, 105-6, 118-19, 123, 125
Blois, 14, 52, 80, 106
Bourbon, Antoine de, 7, 79, 88, 104-5, 108, 111, 113-14, 120, 126
Bourbon, Antoinette de, 86, 111
Bourbon, Henri de. *See* Henri IV.

Bourbon, Louis de (Prince de Condé), 7, 79, 94, 104, 106, **110-17**
Bourbon dynasty, 38
Briçonnet II, Guillaume (bishop), 2-4, 18-19, 24-25, 31, 38-39
Budé, Guillaume, 32-33, 39

Calvin, John, vii, ix-x, 3-5, 8, 10, 17, 21, 23, 27-30, 36, 38-40, 44, **48-63**, 64, 66-68, 70, 78, 84-87, 89-94, 99, 102, 105, 107, 113, 115, 118-19
Calvinism (Calvinist), vii, ix, 21, 59, 86-87, 91, 100, 103, 108, 111, 128
Caroli, Pierre, 3, 27, 54-55, 58, 67
Castellio, Sebastian, 60-62
Catherine de Medici, 6, 8-9, 14, 20, 45-46, 78-79, 81, 85-86, 88, 94, 97, 105-9, 112-15, 119-21, 127-28
Catholic Church, ix, 1, 3, 5-6, 17, 19-21, 24, 26, 28, 30, 37-38, 40, 44, 51, 59, 68, 77, 88, 105, 108, 113, 118, 124, 127, 130, 133-35
Catholicism, 1, 4, 12-15, 21, 30, 33, 59, 65, 81, 84, 88, 94, 105, 107, 109, 123, 125, 127, 129, 131, 134
Catholic League, 13-14, 47, 116, 129, 131
Chandieu, Antoine de, vii, 91, **118-25**
Charlemagne, 7, 71
Charles V, 39, 43-44, 53, 85, 100, 104, 111
Charles VIII, 38

INDEX

Charles IX, 8–9, 12, 42, 47, 82, 86, 88, 94–95, 97–98, 101, 108–9, 113, 115–16, 119, 122, 127–28
Charles de Bourbon (constable), 42–43
Charles de Louviers, 81
Cicero, 32, 50, 72–73, 97
Circle (Group) of Meaux, 3, 19–20
Clement VII (pope), 20, 25
Clément Marot, 4, 6, 36, 38, 40, 55, 86
Coligny, Gaspard de, vii, 8, 10–11, 32, 77–83, 85, 89, 95–96, 107, 109, 113–16, 120–21, 128–29 134
Concordat (Bologna 1516), 18
Confession of Faith, 5, 27–28, 54, 87, 111, 121, 129
Council of Trent, 9, 44, 99, 108, 127

Diego Laynez, 10, 95
Diet of Worms, 19
Dragonnades, 134

Edict of Amboise, 97, 107, 114, 116
Edict of Beaulieu, 139
Edict of Boulogne, 139
Edict of Compiègne, 4
Edict of Écouen, 111
Edict of Fontainebleau. *See* Revocation of the Edict of Nantes.
Edict (Peace) of Longjumeau, 116, 123, 139
Edict of Nantes, ix, 15, 84, 92, 130–34
Edict of Nemours, 139
Edict of Romorantin, 9, 98
Edict of Saint-Germain (Edict of January), 4, 46, 88, 96, 99, 106, 113, 127
Edict of Toleration, 136
Elizabeth I, 89, 114, 138
England, 44, 76, 89, 105, 111, 133–35
Erasmus, 2–3, 17–18, 32–38, 50, 52–53, 137
Estates-General, 9, 14, 45, 99, 112, 120
Etienne Dolet, 32

Farel, Guillaume, x, 3, 5, 19, 23–30, 36, 39, 52–56, 59, 62, 65–67, 84–85, 119

Fontainebleau, 8, 75, 95, 113, 134
François I, 4, 18, 20, 28, 32, 34–40, 42
François II, 5, 7–9
François d'Andelot, 78, 120
François de Morel, 119
French Revolution, 136

Gallican, 9, 87, 98–99
Gastines, Philippe de, 11, 81, 83
Geneva, 2, 5, 7–8, 23, 26–27, 29, 49, 52–56, 58, 60–63, 65, 67–69, 75–76, 84–87, 89–91, 94, 107, 119, 123–25
Germany, ix, 1, 29, 35, 76, 90–91, 125
Guise, François de, 8, 85, 95, 106–7, 110, 112–14, 128
Guise, Henri de, 129
Guise, House of, 45, 78, 80, 86–87, 94, 111

Heinrich Bullinger, 52, 62
Henri II, 4, 6, 20, 58, 73–74, 78–79, 85–86, 94, 98, 103–5, 110–12, 119, 126–27
Henri III, 12–14, 38, 82, 111, 115, 124–27, 129
Henri IV (Henri de Navarre), ix, 10, 12–13, 14–15, 37–38, 80–81, 84, 90, 104, 108–9, 116, 124–25, 126–32, 133–34
Henry VIII (England), 44, 111
Huguenots, vii, ix, 1, 5, 10–12, 15, 40–41, 45–47, 71, 80, 82–83, 86, 88, 94–99, 101, 104, 106, 109, 112–14, 121, 124, 127, 130, 135

Inquisition, 9, 44, 60, 107
Institutes of the Christian Religion, 5, 51
Ippolito (Hippolyte) d'Este, 9–10, 95, 99

Jacques d'Ablon, 8, 95
Jacques Clément, 14, 129
Jean Vallières, 34
Jérôme Aléandre, 32
Jérôme Bolsec, 58
Jesuits, 138, 140
Julius II (pope), 34, 107

152

INDEX

Justification by faith, 6, 18, 35, 39, 136

La Place, Pierre de, **93–102**
La Rochelle, 40, 90, 100, 109, 116, 123, 128, 133–33
Lausanne, 5, 54, 63–64, 66–68, 85–86, 119, 123–24, 136
Lefèvre, Jacques (d'Étaples), vii, 1, 3–4, 17–**22**, 24–25, 31, 33, 35, 38–40, 49
Lord's Supper, 5, 11, 55, 57, 62, 67, 79, 84, 90, 105, 119, 128, 130
L'Hôpital, Michel de, 1, 9, **42–47**, 88, 95, 98–99, 113
Louis IX, 104, 110
Louis XII, 38–39, 111
Louis XIII, 15, 132–34
Louis XIV, 15, 132, 134–35
Louis XVI, 135
Louis de Tillet, 51
Louis Ruzé, 33
Lutherans, ix, 2–3, 20–21, 31–35, 40, 45, 49, 52, 55, 62, 84, 86, 90
Luther, Martin, ix, 3, 17–19–20, 23, 25, 34, 36, 38–39, 44, 61–62

Marguerite de Valois (Navarre), 1, 4, 21, **37–41**, 44, 50, 103, 110
Mathurin Cordier, 48, 85
Meaux, 2–3, 12, 19–20, 24–25, 28, 38, 42, 46, 106, 130
Medici, Catherine de, 6–9, 14, 20, 45–46, 78–79, 81, 85–86, 88, 94, 97, 105–9, 112–15, 119–21, 127–28
Medici, Marie de, 131, 133–34
Melanchthon, Philip, 34, 55, 62, 85
Mérindol massacre, 28–29
Montauban, 124, 128, 133

Navarre, Henri de. *See* Henri IV.
Nérac, 21, 39–40, 107, 125
Nicholas Cop, 20–21, 40, 50, 52
Ninety-Five Theses, 19
Notre Dame Cathedral, 36

Oecolampadius, 25, 52

Paul III (pope), 38, 44, 104
Peace of Saint-Germain, 11, 80, 101, 128
Philippe II (Spain), 8, 107, 115, 130
Philippe III (Spain), 131
Protestantism, 1, 13, 37–38, 42, 50, 71, 79, 81, 87–88, 91–92, 94, 103, 105, 107–11, 115, 118, 127, 129, 131–32
Purgatory, 3, 6, 20, 24

Queen Elizabeth I, 89, 105

Ramus, Peter, **70–76**,
Reformation, ix, 1–3, 20–23, 25–28, 30–31, 37–38, 40–41, 46, 55, 61, 64–66, 78, 84–85, 87, 89, 92, 105, 110–11, 113, 115–18, 134
Reformed Church(es), 5, 23, 69, 78, 87, 89, 111, 118, 121, 125, 135
Religion Prétendue Réformée, 131
Revocation of the Edict of Nantes, 15, 134–35
Rome, 6, 17, 18, 20, 32, 43, 56, 86–87, 90–91, 130

Saint Bartholomew's Day massacre, ix, 71, 76, 90, 93, 101, 109, 121, 123
Seneca, 50, 53
Servetus, Michael, x, 59–60, 62, 91
Sorbonne, 5, 14, 21, 24, 31–32, 34–35, 39–40, 87
Switzerland, 1, 21, 25, 40, 64–65, 76, 91, 125, 135
Synods, 111, 121, 123, 136
Synod of Dordt, 91

Third Estate, 14, 98
Treaty of Fleix, 124
Treaty (Edict) of Nemours, 13

Vassy, Massacre of, ix, 10, 46, 80, 88, 96, 99, 106, 113, 121, 127
Vatican, 168
Vermigli, Peter Martyr, 9, 95
Versailles, 135
Viret, Pierre, 34, 56, **64–69**, 85

INDEX

Waldensians (*Vaudois*), 28–29, 84
Wars of Religion, ix, 20, 47, 71, 75, 77, 83, 88–89, 100–104, 110, 126–27, 131, 134

Wolmar, Melchior, 3, 32, 49, 85
Wittenberg, 25, 39

Zwingli, Ulrich, 19, 25, 52, 62, 112

www.ingramcontent.com/pod-product-compliance
Lightning Source LLC
Chambersburg PA
CBHW051105160426
43193CB00010B/1321